The
Opium-Eating Editor:
Thomas De Quincey
and
The Westmorland Gazette

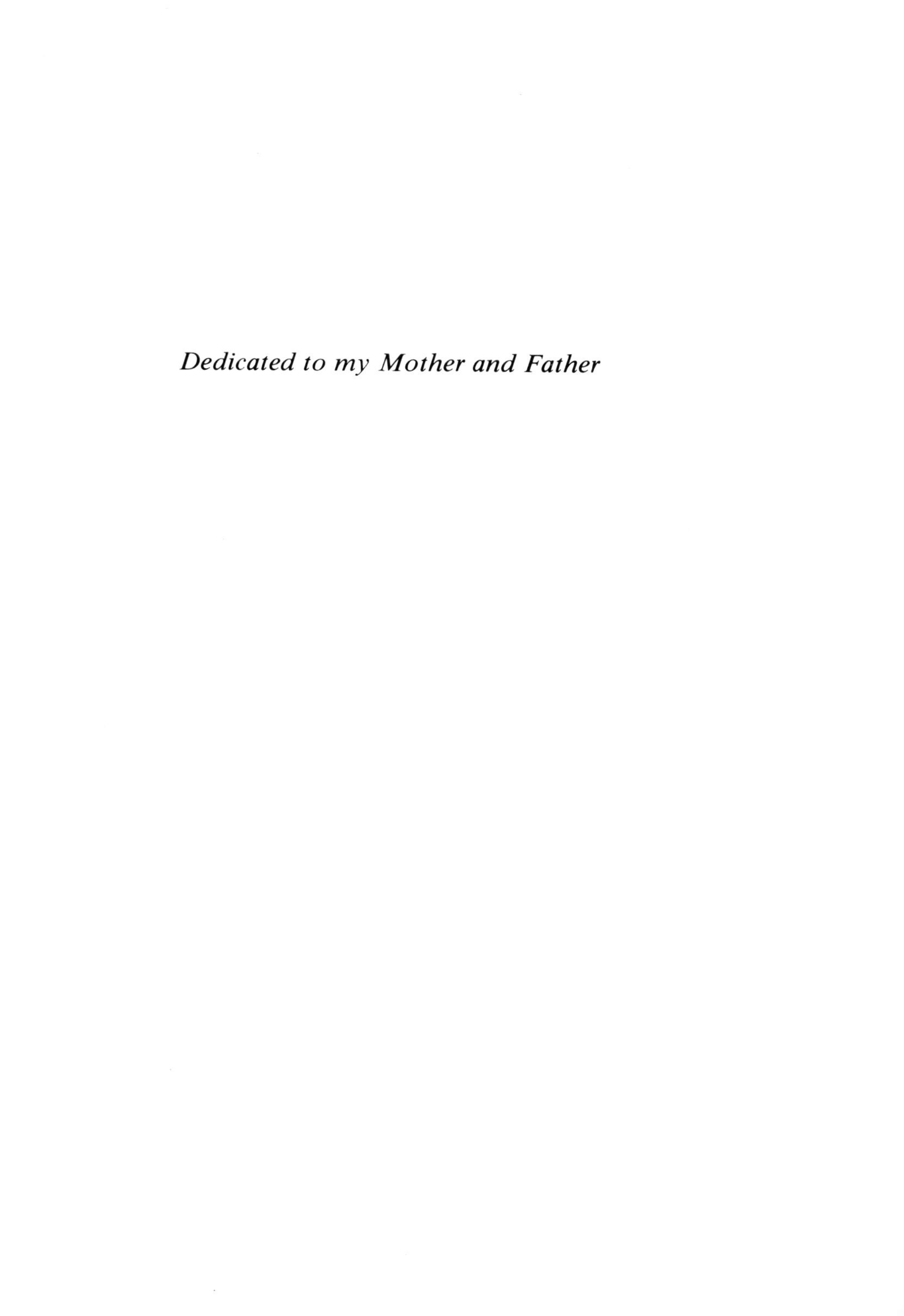

Dedicated to my Mother and Father

Thomas De Quincey,
painting by Sir John Watson Gordon, c.1845.

The Opium-Eating Editor

Thomas de Quincey

and

The Westmorland Gazette,

by Richard Caseby

"O Pegasus roped to a cart. — in the shabbily-paid editorship of a provincial Tory Newspaper."
David Masson.

Westmorland Gazette

First Published June 1985

ISBN No. 0 902272 60 8

Printed and Published in England by Westmorland Gazette,
22 Stricklandgate, Kendal, Cumbria.

Preface

Thomas De Quincey's masterpiece, Confessions of an English Opium-Eater, is the most personal and engaging of autobiographies: it carries the reader on a tide of musical prose through a life of Elysian wonder and devastation. This essay became the best seller that set a fashion for drug abuse among the young and established its author as a top littérateur of his day. Many copied the Confessions' formula, but none matched it. The strength and beauty of the essay lies in De Quincey's highly stylised writing, which can at once be baroque and intimate. At its best, this writing was an attempt to fuse poetry and prose.

Confessions was the voice De Quincey had been long searching for: it suited his self-absorbed, sensitive and feminine nature, and allowed him to illustrate selectively his strange, early life. Above all, Confessions gave De Quincey the chance of revealing himself in the light in which he wanted others to see him — as a tortured, mystical figure who submitted to the bondage of opium. It was a half truth. Only a couple of years before the fame of Confessions, De Quincey was a long way from his ideal of a Romantic hero, ostracised to the fringe of society.

Between 1818 and 1819 De Quincey was Editor of The Westmorland Gazette in Kendal, where he sipped his glass of laudanum and campaigned fiercely against the spread of Radical ideas. Like Wordsworth in later life, De Quincey was a Tory reactionary of the highest order. But sadly, De Quincey's journalism at the Gazette has for years suffered from a bad press. In 1936 the De Quincey biographer Horace Ainsworth Eaton wrote: "His editorship can hardly be called successful." And in 1949 Arthur Aspinall, in his book Politics and the Press, noted: "There can be no doubt of his failure as an editor, even though he did raise the literary character of the paper." One reason for such dismissals is that it is perhaps difficult to reconcile a prose writer of the Romantic movement with anything less than rebellion, political agitation, emotional instability and unworldliness. De Quincey was not exempt from all these traits — he was a poor timekeeper and too eager to justify himself — but he sufficiently recovered his wits to edit a party newspaper that was a commercial and political success. Only very recently have opinions started to change.

Grevel Lindop, in his biography The Opium Eater: A Life of Thomas De Quincey, published in 1981, provides a much needed revision of De Quincey's life in the light of new research: he now acknowledges that De Quincey made "not a bad job" of the Gazette. The authoritative work that has doubtless led to the revision of this period in De Quincey's life is the doctoral dissertation by F. S. Janzow, of the University of Chicago, called De Quincey Enters Journalism: His Contributions to The Westmorland Gazette 1818 — 1819, which endeavours to identify all De Quincey's articles in the Gazette. I owe a great debt to Dr. Janzow for providing an invaluable guide during the reading of all those faded and brittle newspapers.

My book is a small addition to the growing store of evidence for the defence of De Quincey as Editor. It necessarily draws on De Quincey's childhood, but only to put the preoccupations of his adult life into perspective. The heart of the book sets De Quincey's Editorship within a political context against the background of a complicated relationship with Wordsworth. Some hitherto unpublished Lowther family correspondence shows the extent to which the ruling county gentry used Wordsworth as a political spy and intermediary in its dealings with the Gazette. These letters also reveal the attempts at editorial interference, which De Quincey so readily fended off, or ignored. The book contains extracts from The Westmorland Gazette, which illustrate De Quincey's range of obsessions and interests, from his attitude towards journalism to his fascination for murders. Finally, The Danish Origin of the Lake Country Dialect, first published in the Gazette in the

Autumn of 1819, is reprinted in full. "Mr. Wordsworth may do me a favour," wrote De Quincey, "to accept it as an appendix to his work on the English Lakes." But Wordsworth never did. It only seems just that the full version should at last find an audience.

De Quincey stood out in a crowd despite his slight stature. He had fine features lit up with a "hectic glow" (from opium or hiking?) and walked briskly about his business, moving neither arms nor head. His clothes were always ancient and he often peered out at the world from under a hat perched on the back of his head. Had he paused to speak to you, you would have been astonished at his gentle eloquence — an eloquence that graced all his conversation and, on occasion, the pages of the Gazette. Even after a bad day at the office he could decorate a most commonplace emotion with vivid whimsy: ". . . he has fervently wished that some Eastern magician would, a few hours before publication, loosen the 'Gazette' Office from that rock on which we trust it is built — raise it into the air with all its live and dead stock — and would transport it for one week, — not (as angry people are apt to say) into the Red Sea, but to some comfortable place on its shore, Arabia Felix for instance, where the 'Gazette' — falling among those to whom it would speak an unknown tongue — might pass for a learned commentary on the Koran; the price of eggs and butter in the Kendal market might pass for a calculation of eclipses, with a mystical prophecy of wrath to come against the Wechabites; and the Editor's own essays, instead of being torn to pieces by Q's and P.Q's might be stored up among the religious archives at Meccha as an object of devotional reverence to all faithful Musselmen, and a means of kindling polemics among the learned Mohammedan doctors. A fate such as this, or any fate that would have saved his papers from misconstruction, the Editor has many times wished to the 'Gazette', when it became too late to recall what he had sent."

This man, a provincial newspaper Editor in a country market town, betrayed his meek strangeness whenever he spoke or wrote. He is certainly worthy of close acquaintance and better justice than passing dismissal. Seventy-one years after De Quincey resigned, a successor to the chair, Charles Pollitt, wrote an affectionate memoir on the opium-eater's Editorship and scorned the "literary heresy" of De Quincey as a failure. Time again, I think, for a fresh look.

I am indebted to the Trustees of Dove Cottage, the Earl of Lonsdale, The Westmorland Gazette and Kendal and Carlisle Records Offices. I am most grateful to Dr. Robert Woof, secretary to the Trustees of Dove Cottage, and Dr. Terry McCormick, resident curator of the Wordsworth Museum, for their help and guidance. Special thanks to Jo for reading the proofs and, of course, for her encouragement.

Richard Caseby,
Kendal, December 1984.

Contents

Chapter		Page
1	Girlish Tears	13
2	On the Road	28
3	Greeting the Dark Interpreter	42
4	For Better or Worse	62
5	Government Property and High Tories	85
6	Newspaper at War	118
7	The Babbling Garrulity of Daylight	147
	Epilogue	162
	Appendix: The Danish Origin of the Lake Country Dialect	165
	Bibliography	186
	References	189

List of Illustrations

Frontispiece Thomas De Quincey, painting by Sir John Watson Gordon, c.1845 (National Portrait Gallery)

Town End, Grasmere 107

Kate Wordsworth's grave, Grasmere 108

Thomas De Quincey's opium scales, Town End . . 109

Election poster, (Cumbria Records Office, Kendal) . . 110

Election poster, (Cumbria Records Office, Kendal) . . 111

Engraving of a Stanhope Press 112

Notice of dissatisfaction with the first Gazette Editor (Cumbria Records Office) 113

Thomas De Quincey, detail from chalk sketch by James Archer RSA, 1855 114

Letter to De Quincey's uncle about Gazette Editorship (Cumbria Records Office, Kendal) 115

Draft of Gazette article by De Quincey (Cumbria Records Office, Kendal) 116

Page of Gazette accounts book, The Westmorland Gazette 117

Chapter One
Girlish Tears

> *"Childhood is measured out by sounds and smells,*
> *And sights, before the dark of reason grows."*
> *John Betjeman, Summoned by Bells.*

Thomas De Quincey was made in childhood. He felt that period with a peculiar intensity and it dominated his life's writing, if not consciously, then at a more sublime level. Unlike Marcel Proust, who tried to portray life in art by means of memory shaping and moulding the past, De Quincey gave us a shadowy and evasive offering. If petite madeleine crumbs in a spoonful of tea could trigger off Proust's involuntary stream of childhood memories of Combray, then all De Quincey needed was a dose of laudanum to evoke his early years with piercing clarity and unpredictable emphasis. The medium suited the man. De Quincey was a haunted reader and writer who loved to chase the things that disturbed or even terrified him. This was a habit he never lost, and it started in his childhood.

De Quincey was born on August 15th, 1785, the child of Elizabeth Penson, who was married, rather below her social station, to Thomas Quincey, a linen merchant from Boston, in Lincolnshire. Two years before Thomas junior was born, Mr. Quincey quit retail trade in Manchester to become a merchant rather than a shopkeeper. It was a step up in the world.

The family lived in a house at Deansgate, in Manchester, but soon after Thomas was born they moved to The Farm, at Moss Side, in open country. The sickly little boy had immediate companions: sisters Elizabeth two years his senior and Mary one year his senior, and the first born, his brother William. But they did not provide the friction and toughening expected of a large, lively family. His brother waited some years before presenting him with those gifts.

From the age of two to four Thomas was ill with an "ague" and at three he suffered an attack of whooping cough. He was petted and cossetted by his sisters and he submitted willingly to this soft, maternal shield, which his real mother never granted him. Thomas remembered with some longing that his "infant feelings were moulded by the gentlest of sisters and not by horrid pugilistic brothers."[1]

As a child being prepared for a long journey, Thomas recalled: "Outside her door, however, there awaited me some silly creatures, women, of course, old and young, from the nursery and the kitchen, who gave, and who received, those fervent kisses which wait only upon love without awe and without disguise. Heavens! what rosaries might be strung for the memory of sweet female kisses, given without check or art, before one is of an age to value them! And again, how sweet is the touch of female hands as they array one for a journey!"[2]

He was shy, sensitive and claimed he began a lifetime of reverie at a startlingly precocious age. Thomas recalled a dream of "terrific grandeur" when he was two years old about one of his favourite nurses. This he holds as evidence that his dreaming tendencies were "constitutional and not dependant upon laudanum,"[3] although in those days an elixir was often given to children who had colds and the substance did contain a small amount of the drug. However, De Quincey says the elixir was never administered except under medical supervision: it is likely that the emotional security woven by his sisters was far more intoxicating for the frail youngster than a rare sup of syrup. This relationship with the sisters was certainly not one-sided; Thomas loved in return with a passion that was too soon crippled by bereavement.

Whatever the cause of Thomas' dreams, they continued. He sensed a deep feeling of pathos at an image he conjured up of early flowering crocuses. At the other extreme he had a recurring reverie about lying down in front of a lion, a terrifying act he committed with the irresistible compulsion only to be found in a nightmare. If Hercules wrestling with a lion signifies a tussle with the physical side of human nature, how could Thomas' submission be construed? Certainly a lack of will was a hallmark of his adult years, but were the die really cast in infancy? De Quincey thought so.

By the time Thomas was five his father's business was healthy enough for the family to contemplate moving house once more. Greenhay was built made-to-measure in three acres near Moss Side. The family had now grown with the addition of four-year-old Jane, who died the year of the move, Richard aged one, and a new baby, Jane. Thomas was unwilling to relinquish his position as the focus of attention as the youngest Quincey, and even in later life he called the surviving Jane his "older" sister.

His security was threatened by the death of the elder Jane. Thomas was four and a half years old and her loss left him in "sad perplexity" with a vague feeling that she might return. This confusion was aggravated by rumours that a female servant had brutally treated her just before her death. The boy was frightened.

"If there was one thing in this world from which, more than any other, nature had forced me to revolt," recalled Thomas, "it was brutality and violence."[4]

Two years later his beloved sister Elizabeth fell ill with fever. And within days her condition was so serious that the other children were not allowed to see her. Elizabeth's death was a blow from which Thomas never fully recovered and for the rest of his life he had a paralysing fear of her illness, hydrocephalus or cerebro-spinal meningitis. Elizabeth had shown Thomas unstinting love and had been closest to his most private imaginative worlds. No longer would she care for him, read with him or play nursery games: Thomas had lost his mother.

The last time he saw her was on the afternoon of her death. Thomas stole into the room from which he was barred. He softly closed the door.

"Then, turning round, I sought my sister's face. But the bed had been moved, and the back was now turned towards myself.

Nothing met my eyes but one large window, wide open, through which the sun of mid-summer at mid-day was showering torrents of splendour. The weather was dry, the sky was cloudless, the blue depths seemed the express types of infinity; and it was not possible for eye to behold, or for heart to conceive, any symbols more pathetic of life and the glory of life."

When he turned from the sunlight to the corpse he saw Elizabeth's "marble lips" and the "stiffening hands, laid palm to palm." He stood checked in quivering awe; the sound of a summer wind breathing outside reached his ears and he fell into a trance.

"A vault seemed to open in the zenith of the far blue sky which ran up forever. I, in spirit, rose as if on billows that also ran up the shaft forever; and the billows seemed to pursue the throne of God . . ."

In this state Thomas imagined "some mighty relation between God and death," which "dimly struggled to evolve itself." And time, for a while, stopped. Thomas wavered in the suspension and only recovered when he thought he heard a foot on the stairs.

"Hastily, therefore, I kissed the lips that I should kiss no more, and slunk, like a guilty thing, with steps from the room. Thus perished the vision, loveliest among all the shows which earth has revealed to me; thus mutilated was the parting which should have lasted forever; tainted thus with fear that farewell sacred to love and grief, to perfect love and to grief that could not be healed." [5]

He returned the following day but the key had been taken from the lock. This final bar was a mercy: doctors had already performed an autopsy on Elizabeth's brain. At the funeral Thomas' desire to mourn openly was frustrated by adults who worried over etiquette and failed to understand his depth of feeling: they told him to hold a white handkerchief to his eyes while in church. Thomas' hyperbolic rant and his retrospective contempt for such "masks or mockeries," rival Hamlet's at Ophelia's graveside.

"Fifty thousand sneering faces would not have troubled me

now in any office of tenderness to my sister's memory. Ten legions would not have repelled me from seeking her, if there had been a chance that she could be found." [6]

Now Thomas actively sought solitude and created a private world that could not be touched by cruel reality. He was taunted for his "girlish tears" and discouraged from showing further grief. Withdrawal was complete, and the jagged resentment was buried away from the eyes of others. Children are quick to read others and when a parent is afraid of exhibiting feeling, children will hide their own. What Thomas needed was a secure relationship with his mother, prompt and accurate information about Elizabeth's death and the chance to play a full part in the family funeral rites. He was denied all these channels of mourning. As a result, he developed fears about his own death and a deep sadness, which contributed to a lifelong depressive condition.

Mrs. Quincey was not warm to her children and either refused or was genuinely unable to show them spontaneous affection. Without gentle coaxing, there was little chance of Thomas initiating a thaw.

"For I was the shyest of children; and, at all stages of life a natural sense of personal dignity held me back from exposing the least ray of feeling which I was not encouraged wholly to reveal." [7]

When Thomas did talk, he seemed incapable of brevity; consequently, he was cut or misunderstood by his impatient mother, whose evangelist tendencies were revealed by her stress on discipline. Mrs. Quincey hoped to quash any conceit in her offspring, and even when she met the boy protégé Macaulay, her admiration was qualified with, "but he says such extraordinary things that he will be ruined by praise."[8]

Soon after the move to Greenhay, the tubercular Mr. Quincey gained a new partnership that enabled him to pursue sun and health in the West Indies. He was not seen again until he came home to die. William, the eldest son, was sent to boarding school almost as soon as he was six while Thomas remained at home in female company. At Greenhay, Thomas' first delight was the library which embraced books on travel, voyages, history, biography and belles-lettres. His favourite book was Arabian Nights, and after the nurse had read to him from the large illustrated edition, the exotic scenes conspired to cram his dreams with romance and fear — even in adult life.

But Thomas soon recognised the library's shortcomings, and he came to regard it as "a poor library . . . for a scholar or a man of research. Its use and purpose was mere enjoyment, instant amusement without effort or affectation." [9] It was fitting. Mr. Quincey was a plain, yet thoughtful man, who was a founder member of the Manchester Literary and Philosophical Society, and had published a book entitled Short Tour in the Midland Counties of England. He was upright and respectable, although Thomas recalled: "Nobody, that I remember, praised him under the notion of a clever man, or a man of talent." [10] On the other hand, Thomas was showing a prodigious intellect. By the age of eight he was already spending all his weekly allowance on books and was even in debt to a bookseller for three guineas. Throughout his life, as he beavered to amass an impressive library, such debts followed in an untidy wake. As for his inaugural debt, Thomas worried about it for three years before he discovered that the bookseller had charged his tutor. Worry, of course, formed niggling eddies trailing behind the debts. It was a vicious circle from which Thomas was seldom free.

Mr. Quincey came home in 1793 and died of tuberculosis. To Thomas, the sick forty-year-old was a stranger; but father and son had a few weeks to get to know each other. After Mr. Quincey's death, William was brought home from Louth Grammar School, where he had been hardened into a survivor and twelve-year-old adventurer. Life took a sharp change for Thomas.

William was a despot who despised Thomas for his cowardice and inadequate physique. He detested books, but wrote his own on anything from magic and pyrotechnics to necromancy. His brothers and sisters provided an unwilling, yet captive audience for his frequent lectures. In short, William was a whirlwind in the stuffy safety of Greenhay. Although Thomas retreated from his boisterous teacher, he eventually reacted with a pathological love for the contempt that was lavished on him. It was his peculiar way of enjoying the new excitement.

"But it happened . . . that I had a perfect craze for being despised. I doted on it; and considered contempt a sort of luxury that I was in continual fear of losing. . ." [11]

William was certainly a live-wire. He made a hot-air balloon from which the family cats made their first successful parachute jumps, and he contrived a humming-top machine that was supposed to enable him to stand on the ceiling. Thomas remembered dryly: "The apparatus for spinning him, however, perhaps from its complexity, would not work; a fact evidently owing to the stupidity of the gardener." [12]

Slanging matches and brawls with local factory lads were soon initiated by William, who press-ganged Thomas as his terrified deputy in an army of two. Back at camp, William issued a bi-weekly newspaper detailing false victories with the gay abandon of the most unscrupulous of propagandists. Libel was rife, and all of it was directed at the somewhat bewildered Thomas. It was his first taste of journalism, albeit a bitter one.

"I suppose no creature ever led such as life as I did in that gazette. Run up to the giddiest heights of promotion on one day, for merits which I could not myself discern, in a week or two I was brought to a court martial for offences equally obscure."[13]

The two brothers were taught by the Rev. Samuel Hall, of Salford, who was also one of their guardians upon the death of Mr. Quincey. Latin and Greek were the staple diet, and Thomas soon revealed his gift for languages. On Sundays the boys heard the lazy minister preach — he had about 300 sermons that revolved in a three year cycle — and Thomas was forced to memorise his boring tracts. The Monday tests left the youngster "under sad anticipation" on Saturday, and on Sunday night his "pillow was stuffed with thorns." He found the tasks difficult because he thought Hall's train of thought arbitrary, and as a result the confused sermons invaded his dreams and left him with a lifelong hatred of learning by rote. Hall once even tried to get his pupil to memorise the dictionary from A to Z. Thomas refused.

In the Hall household Thomas met two odd young daughters of the minister who were despised by their mother and kept as servants. He deliberately sought them out and offered friendship.

"Gradually, however, I came to be aware of their forlorn condition, to pity them, and to love them. The poor twins were undoubtedly plain, to a degree which is called, by unfeeling people, ugliness. They were also deaf, as I have said, and they were scrofulous; one of them was disfigured by the small-pox; they had glimmering eyes, red, like the eyes of ferrets, and scarcely half-open; and they did not so much walk as stumble along. There, you have the worst of them. Now, hear something on the other side." [14]

The other side was their affection for each other "united in their constant sadness" and Thomas' notion that they were destined for an early death. Thomas kissed the girls in greeting — probably the only stranger to do so — and they responded with grateful smiles for the pupil who denied their repulsiveness. The twins' mother merely saw them as creatures who disgraced her — but not for long. Thomas' notion, inspired by a confused connexion with Elizabeth's death, was proved right. The girls died of scarlet fever in 1797. Their memory remained with Thomas, as did his acutely sensitive feeling for his fellow man. The oppressed, miserable or slighted, attracted both his curiosity and pity, and reinforced his melancholic bent.

When it came to William's dares, Thomas could rarely resist. He had nothing to prove — natural boyish pride was non-existent and the chance of rising in his brother's esteem was nil — but he consistently cast himself in the role of victim to discover a fluttering terror with every ingenious trick invented by William. The garden swing at a friend's house was a prime example of Thomas' delicious torment.

"Horror was at my heart regularly as the swing reached its most aeriel altitude; for the oily, swallow-like fluency of the swoop downwards threatened always to make me sick, in which case it is probable that I must have relaxed my hold of the ropes, and have been projected, with fatal violence, to the ground. But in defiance of all this miserable panic, I continued to swing whenever he tauntingly invited me." [15]

One of the last experiences with William was the sighting of a rabid dog on the other side of a brook. The slavering beast from a nearby horse barracks had bitten two horses and several soldiers. With characteristic aplomb, William beckoned the dog to leap the strip of water whilst threatening to crown it if the challenge was accepted. Thomas could only stare. A few seconds later a rabble of pursuers armed with pitchforks and carbines chased and killed the dog.

Thomas was relieved when William was sent to study drawing and painting under the fashionable artist P. J. de Loutherbourg RA. "It was well that my brother's path in life soon ceased to coincide with my own," wrote Thomas, "else I should infallibly have broken my neck in confronting perils which brought me neither honour nor profit." [16] Their paths never coincided again. William suffered an attack of typhus and died at de Loutherbourg's Hammersmith home in November 1797.

When Mrs. Quincey decided that Greenhay was too expensive to run, the family moved to Bath in 1796. Leaving Greenhay was dear. The house was sold for little over one third of the cost price, and marked the first of many similar, ill-advised business decisions by Mrs. Quincey. Her greatest infirmity, as Thomas remarked, was "the costly one of seeking her chief intellectual excitement in architectural creations."[17]

Thomas and his younger brother Richard, nicknamed 'Pink' on account of his rosy complexion, stayed on to study under Hall while their mother settled at the spa town. Thomas eventually entered Bath Grammar School at the age of twelve, and there his talent for Greek and Latin was honed to a degree that prompted the headmaster to say to a friend: "That boy could harangue an Athenian mob better than you or I could address an English one." Such exceptional ability did not endear Thomas to his fellow pupils, who resented teachers "throwing in their teeth" [18] the brilliance of his verses.

Thomas' promising career at the school was brought to an unfortunate end when a master accidentally missed caning a disobedient boy, and swiped Thomas instead. Thomas left school with a suspected fractured skull, which one doctor talked of curing by trepanning. But he only convalesced at home to nurse both his sore head and obsessional interest in his own health. He was not yet a hypochondriac, but he always had a "nervous panic" about sickness, which was stirred by his memories of Elizabeth's death. While Thomas lay wrapped and worried, Mrs. Quincey read him a translation of Ariosto's Orlando Furioso — the complete work.

Thomas joined Pink at Winkfield School, in Wiltshire, after a short spell under a French tutor. It was at that time that Mrs. Quincey changed the family name to 'De Quincey' perhaps in response to the demands of fashionable Bath society or the tradition that the family was originally descended from the French De Quincis line.[19] Whatever the reason, the name stuck.

At Winkfield, Thomas found no challenge. In a school of thirty boys he was intellectual champion, and the headmaster was in a "perpetual state of panic" lest the star pupil should expose his ignorance. Lack of stimulus in class led Thomas to write for the boys' weekly newspaper, The Observer, and enter translation competitions. It was the only way to escape the numbing crush of boredom.

In 1799 Thomas discovered a new poet who was to exert the most profound influence on his life — William Wordsworth. He read 'We are Seven' from a manuscript circulating in Bath and, naturally, the tale of an eight-year-old cottage girl — who had seen a brother and sister buried, touched a deep chord. Just over two years later he read 'Ruth' in a London newspaper. During this period Thomas was writing his own verses and planned to write a "poetic and pathetic" ballad on the wanderings of a brother and sister who perish after falling asleep on a moonlit, frosty night. Another poem was to describe the emotions of a shipwrecked man washed up on a rock. Neither subject strayed far from the ideals set out in Wordsworth's Preface to the Lyrical Ballads.

In 1800 Thomas set off on a summer holiday to Ireland with young Lord Westport, son of the Irish peer Lord Altmont, whose acquaintance Mrs. De Quincey had cultivated with deliberation. Obviously, Mrs. De Quincey experienced little difficulty in reconciling her determination to establish a social launching pad for her offspring with her evangelist morality. The widow worked hard for her children.

The holiday heralded Thomas' first visit to London, a city which exerted a frightening attraction.

"Finally, for miles before you reach a suburb of London such as Islington, for instance, a last great sign and augury of the immensity which belongs to the coming metropolis forces itself upon the dullest observer, in the growing sense of his own utter insignificance . . . No loneliness can be like that which weighs upon the heart in the centre of faces never-ending, without voice or utterance for him; eyes innumerable, that have 'no speculation' in their orbs which he can understand; and hurrying figures of men and women weaving to and fro, with no apparent purposes intelligible to a stranger, seeming like a mask of maniacs, or, oftentimes, like a pageant of phantoms."[20]

England's Babylon with all its confusion, noise and crude pulse of life cast a spell over Thomas and ensured his return on more enlightening lone sorties. But those experiences lay in the future. His trip with Lord Westport featured a visit to The Whispering Gallery in St. Paul's, a common enough tourist venue but one which fascinated the sensibilities of the precocious Thomas.

At Eton the boys attended a ball at Frogmore, but to Thomas the spectacle only presented a sad symbol of temporality. His isolation and acutely melancholic vision seemed tied inextricably to memories of "masks or mockeries". It should have been a carefree occasion.

". . . such a scene presents a sort of mask of human life, with its hours of golden youth, and the interminable revolution of ages hurrying after ages, and one generation treading upon the flying footsteps of another; whilst all the while the overruling music attempers the mind to the spectacle, the subject to the object, the beholder to the vision."[21]

Thomas could not see without moving to universal symbols.

It was a rare gift, or perhaps affliction, which was to increase his detachment the further he left childhood behind.

The Irish trip started with an early promise of educative and interesting experiences. During the voyage from Holyhead to Kingstown it was so warm that Thomas and Lord Westport bedded on deck within sight of a carriage where a beautiful woman was sleeping. In the middle of the night a man stole to the door of the carriage and entered; the boys' first thought was to raise the alarm, but they were checked by the sight of the door opening from within. Lady Conyngham, later the mistress of George IV, was accepting a lover. Next morning she emerged "looking as beautiful and hardly less innocent than an angel,"[22] whereupon Thomas received his second shock on learning that she was also a wife and mother. Thomas, aged sixteen, was losing his innocence if only by proxy.

In Ireland the boys visited Dublin before travelling to Lord Altmont's estate at Westport, in County Mayo. Thomas saw his host installed as one of the Six Knights of Saint Patrick in Dublin Cathedral, and compared accounts of the Irish Rebellion. His established interest in history gave him a fairly safe footing in the mire of Irish politics, and he relished the opportunity of studying the aftermath of the rebellion at first hand. He remarked that the Irish "speak of it as we should of a Birmingham riot." Perhaps more illuminating was his comment on conflicting English and Irish reports: "The former view it with a magnifying glass, the latter with a microscope."[23]

During the social round, Thomas was bewitched by the twenty-year-old Miss Blake with whom he discussed English poets. He reacted to the flirtation with typical intensity and noted: "From this day I was an altered creature, never again relapsing into the careless, irreflective mind of childhood." His attitude to women was unexceptional for the era. He revered images he had created with little reference to reality; they were myths of angelic virtues which could only stifle the objects of his desire. A pedestal of "exaggerated adoration and insulting intellectual neglect"[24] was the fashion of Thomas' generation, and the teenager was not one to swim against the tide.

The emotion felt for Miss Blake evaporated with the rapidity with which it had appeared. De Quincey's first and only marriage set off on a far different footing, and the unlikely partners managed to settle to the familiar pattern of accepted marital harmony. But for the moment the boy had fantasies.

Thomas left the Irish estate with Lord Westport in early September, and they travelled back to England. Westport and Thomas never met again, though the young Lord found another literary figure to act as companion. He supped and whored with Byron in 1808.

Thomas spent a couple of months at Lord Carbery's seat at Laxton, in Northamptonshire, while his mother and guardians considered the next stage of his education. He enjoyed the library of 17,000 volumes and saw an original quarto edition of Godwin's Political Justice "with all its virus as yet undiluted of raw anti-social Jacobinism."[25] Other diversions included the beautiful, twenty-six-year-old Lady Carbery, who submitted to Thomas' desire to teach her Greek. Meanwhile, a family dispute raged over Thomas' next move. He was a motivated young man who resented the imposition of school and wanted to travel and study on his own before entering university. "Once the petty round of school tasks had been felt as a molestation," said Thomas, "but now, at last, as a degradation."[26] He was too used to the intelligent conversation of distinguished adults who accepted him as an equal. But Mrs. De Quincey brushed aside his shower of objections and sent him to Manchester Grammar School.

"Misgivingly I went forwards, feeling forever that, through clouds of darkness, I was continually nearing a danger, or was myself perhaps wilfully provoking a trial, before which my constitutional despondency would cause me to lie down without a stuggle."[27]

Despite this tone of fatalism, which forever dogged him and is reminiscent of his earliest lion dream, Thomas was soon to show himself an assertive adolescent who was fully prepared to change the direction of his life by an act of outright rebellion against his mother and guardians. For a boy unadventurous by nature, it was a major turning point.

He was enrolled at Manchester Grammar by the Rev. Hall, and the High Master Charles Lawson examined Thomas by handing him a volume of The Spectator and asking him to translate a couple of pages into Latin. The newcomer entered the top class.

Lawson was a great curiosity. He had taught at the school for about fifty years and persisted in tottering about wearing a black velvet suit with lace ruffles at the wrist, and a well-powdered perruque. "He still had his dying to do; he was in arrear as to that," wrote Thomas, "all else was finished."[28] The comment was callous but true. Thomas found a private room, which did little to abate his habit of solitude, and marked time.

Lady Carbery had moved to Manchester to be near a friend, and her drawing room was open to Thomas several evenings a week. He read Coleridge's Ancient Mariner to her, and she taught him some Hebrew. But Thomas was rudely shocked by Lady Carbery's reaction; she laughed at the finest parts of the poem and called the mariner "an old quiz". Yet later she was to surprise him by spontaneously reciting a passage to a clergyman friend.

Thomas also read the work of Thomas Chatterton, who had published poems written before he was twelve that were so good he had passed them off as the work of an early poet. De Quincey found the idea of abused genius perhaps more appealing than the actual poetry, and the memory of the meteoric boy who ran away from home at sixteen and committed suicide by drinking arsenic at eighteen probably lingered longer than the verses.

When a stalemate was reached in an epic argument of letters between Thomas and Mrs. De Quincey about his bid for an Oxford scholarship he decided to flee. First choice of destination was the Lake District, home of his beloved Wordsworth, but the idea was dropped because of the imposition of turning up on the doorstep a penniless runaway. North Wales was a better bet, especially since he had already seen some of the impressive scenery on his way to Ireland.

He rose at 3.30 a.m. on a cloudless July day and ordered a groom to carry his heavy trunk downstairs. Ironically, the burden slipped from the groom's shoulders and the trunk crashed against the headmaster's door. But Lawson slept on, and Thomas escaped into the real world of action and choice. For someone who had constantly been surrounded by protection and care, Thomas was shedding far more than the killing inertia of school.

Chapter Two
On the Road

"Pain driven to agony, or grief driven to frenzy, is essential to the ventilation of profound natures."
Thomas De Quincey, (Van Doren Stern, 910).

The real world of action and choice soon began to make itself felt with an annoying contingency. A £40 bank draft had been delivered by mistake to Thomas, and the threat of a theft charge hot on his heels threw him into confusion. He had also decided to see his sister Mary before setting off on the Welsh jaunt, but unfortunately she was living with his mother at the Priory, in Chester. It was a fussy beginning to Thomas' leap for freedom.

After a two day hike to the Priory, Thomas was caught lurking about the gardens, and his escapade seemed destined to a lame and premature end. The red herring hints to his school fellows that he was running away to the Lakes had worked well; ironically, it was his sister Mary who led a party on a fruitless 600 mile chase to Ambleside. Back in Chester, Thomas was facing the "formidable artillery" of his mother's displeasure and had little to offer in defence. He paid dearly for the Lakes ploy — it cost him £150 of his patrimony. The long touchpaper of anticipation had burned down to a spluttering anticlimax.

However, Thomas was rescued by his uncle, Colonel Thomas Penson, a worldly and bronzed man serving with the East India Company in Bengal, who was house-guest at the Priory. One of the major industries of the company was the smuggling of vast supplies of opium into China; and when Col. Penson returned to India, he became Superintendent of Military Buildings, a post which attracted fat bribes. If the colourful uncle had ever shared Mrs. De Quincey's moral earnestness, it was by now dishevelled and better suited to a world of adventurous self-interest than domestic upheaval. Not surprisingly, he sympathised with the runaway and even persuaded the family to let Thomas continue his travels with a guinea a week allowance into the bargain.

After social visits to family friends and a stay in Bangor, Thomas wandered the bleak and wild countryside in the unpredictable weather of October. Inns were beyond his purse so he made a canvas tent and occasionally slept in the open to avoid the stuffiness of shelter.

When he was driven indoors, he lodged with whoever would take him and paid for the hospitality with literary skills that extended to writing love letters for peasant girls. Daily fifteen mile rambles improved his health and compensated for the discomforts of flea-ridden beds and animals sharing his dining-room. Nevertheless, it was an aimless and generally lonely life.

Company on the road varied from an astrologer who predicted that Thomas would desert twenty-seven children and have his hair turn red, to a German called De Haren who had been a lieutenant in the British Navy. De Haren taught Thomas some of his mother tongue and introduced him to the work of Jean-Paul Richter, an author who bridged the movements of Sturm und Drang and Romanticism, and whose writings were to influence De Quincey's own literary style.

Lack of money meant that Thomas was forced into "periodical transmigrations" from gentleman-tourist to nomad. The society of inns and hotels was expensive, and the price was increasing before Thomas' very eyes. Wales was opening up to travellers, and the first guidebooks were establishing routes. At the same time, the locals were not slow to take advantage of the new demand for beds and board, and Thomas noted that the price of dinner went up by 500 per cent within two months.

Loneliness, dwindling funds and a perverse desire to shake off his guardians led Thomas to his next blind lunge into the unknown. Approved exile was not enough to satisfy a boy who wanted to provoke a full breach.

"I took a fierce resolution to sacrifice my weekly allowance, to slip my anchor and throw myself in desperation upon London."[2]

The irrational decision is a complete mystery. Although De Quincey analysed the effects of his London episode in scrupulous detail in later writings, he fudged over explaining the causes and insisted he was moved by a strange compulsion. In retrospect, he saw it as a wilful mistake but was really rather pleased by the immensely formative experiences found in the metropolis. So why? Compulsion, of course, was nothing new to De Quincey. It may appear to be a handy throwaway to fatalism in this instance but Thomas was desperately attracted to experiences with the promise of terror.

London had already made a profound impression on him during the visit with Lord Westport, and after Wales the "pageant of phantoms" must have presented itself as the ideal warren for a secret and anonymous life. The appealing romantic image of Chatterton was probably not far away; to an intelligent and imaginative teenager he was the youth rebel of the day. But the reality of emulating his hero was soon to cut the polish of Thomas' fancies and scar the boy beneath.

Thomas spent the night before his advance to London at the Lion Inn of Shrewsbury. His waiting-room between lives was theatrical enough to reflect the drama of his wheeling mind as memories of the expansive ranges of Penmaenmawr, Snowdon and Cader Idris receded and a more ominous landscape loomed. He sat alone for three hours in an empty ballroom.

"But now rose London — sole, dark, infinite — brooding over the whole capacities of my heart."[3]

A storm howled outside while Thomas waited for the early morning coach. It was a period of suspension not unlike the one he had experienced in the bedroom of his sister Elizabeth. And he felt it acutely.

"More than ever I stood upon the brink of a precipice; and the local circumstances around me deepened and intensified these reflections, impressed upon them solemnity and terror, sometimes even horror."[4]

The sad sense of temporality inspired by the ball at Frogmore was evoked again by the "rising tumultuous vision" of the room with its echoing hollowness and evanescent images of dancers' flying feet. Thomas was once more chasing after something that attracted him by the very fear it inspired. The paradox happened in dreams and could be made to happen in life.

"Still, as I turned inwards to the echoing chambers, or outwards to the wild night, I saw London expanding her visionary gates to receive me, like some dreadful mouth of Acheron (Acherontis avari). Thou also, Whispering Gallery! Once again in those moments of conscious and wilful desolation didst to my ear utter monitorial sighs. For once again I was preparing to utter an irrevocable word, to enter upon one of those fatally tortuous paths of which the windings can never be unlinked."[5]

An enveloping sense of elegiac farewell waved over him and heightened his loneliness. Thomas had met it before, and it would come again. The event was no longer accident — if, indeed, it ever had been. He actively sought the experience, and it now became the frank of his character.

In contrast, Thomas' first experience of London was bitterly prosaic although enlivened with a curious splash of Dickensian colour. He hoped to borrow £200 on the security of his patrimony in an effort to free himself from the financial shackle of his guardians. A money lender called Dell passed him on to his furtive agent, Brunell, who lived in a sprawling, dilapidated house on Greek Street, in Soho.

Brunell was a revelation in seedy lowlife. He stole in and out of his gloomy house at all hours, checked callers through a side window and slept at a different address each night to avoid bailiffs. Aliases of Brown and Thomas also helped to cover his illicit tracks.

His business deals were as evasive as his identity and Brunell told Thomas that investigations would have to be made before the money was handed over. Days turned into weeks and still no contract was signed. Thomas moved out of lodgings to escape starvation, and Brunell let him stay at his Greek Street home if only to stop his potential client from freezing to death in doorways.

Brunell had a great enthusiasm for literature and told Thomas he had been forced into legal evasions after the sudden death of his father. Security free loans were now his speciality, and he employed a sulky clerk-cum-minder called Pyement to cheer bad debtors. But there was also another character in this strange little cast.

A ten-year-old girl was already installed in the cold and unfurnished rooms. She was bewildered, frightened and hungering for company. Each night Thomas and the ghostly child huddled together for warmth under a rug while rats rattled and scratched on the stairs and hallway. The girl lived in an emotional vacuum: she had no idea of her parentage, though Thomas suspected that she was the illegitimate daughter of Brunell. Even so, the money lender gave no clues and treated her merely as a servant.

Thomas gave what sympathy and comfort he could, perhaps stirred by the memory of the pitiful Hall daughters, but material comfort was at a premium. Both youngsters were living under severe deprivation and Thomas had to steal scraps from Brunell's breakfast plate to survive. Hunger pains tormented his stomach, and his sleep was a battleground of dreams.

Like true misery, the life was monotonous. A yearning to visit Wordsworth at Grasmere was his only source of spiritual succour during his desultory city wanderings.

In 1802 London was slipping into the first stage of the harrying speed of the industrial revolution. Population and poverty were increasing and an underworld which could turn from comic charm to monstrous hypocrisy and violence was fast developing. Genteel society was defiantly ignorant of this burgeoning street-life, except where the mutually exclusive worlds occasionally met in outrage or disgust. Thomas, however, was submerged in this alien sector of snatch and thrust. The frail boy intellectual who crouched on doorsteps for hours must have screamed 'victim' to the bustle around him. But he was lucky.

"Being myself at that time of necessity a peripatetic, or a walker of the streets, I naturally fell in more frequently with those female peripatetics who are technically called street-walkers. Some of these women had occasionally taken my part against watchmen who wished to drive me off the steps of houses where I was sitting; others had protected me against more serious aggressions. But to one amongst them . . . I owe it that I am at this time alive."[6]

This was Ann, a sixteen-year-old girl forced to the profession after being seduced by a "brutal ruffian". Once, when Thomas collapsed, Ann ran for a glass of port wine and spices to revive him, even though it was a luxury she could ill-afford. The story of wronged innocence in a selfless act makes a neat vignette. Perhaps too neat — Ann is the perfect Romantic image. Virtue in a wistful outcast, who was attracted to a boy out of affection not sex, was De Quincey's ideal. So was Ann really a poetic creation?

It is plausible that a young prostitute should want to adopt Thomas. He was young, small, attractive and had always enjoyed familiar relations with females. His utter helplessness was probably another spur to pity. But Ann is never mentioned by De Quincey outside a strictly literary context and conforms so very easily to an immaculate fantasy. The story can never be proved, but it does appear to align with De Quincey's history of seeking and finding sisterly love.

Finally, Brunell offered £300 on condition that young Lord Westport signed as guarantor. Thomas realised that the money lender wanted the contact rather than the security of the name, and he prepared to travel to Eton. He arranged to meet Ann again five days later at 6 p.m. at the corner of Great Titchfield Street. But during the tearful farewell and rash of promises, Thomas neglected to ask her surname. They never saw each other again.

The expedition was also a failure. Westport had left Eton for

Jesus College, Cambridge, and although Thomas engineered Altamont's cousin as guarantor, Dell refused to forward the loan. Ann never appeared at the rendezvous, so Thomas went in search among the alleys and streets, appealing to the sceptical drifters. The boy's first impression of London proved uncannily apt. The "eyes innumerable that have 'no speculation' in their orbs" gave blank refusal to his desperate questions. With hindsight, De Quincey even enjoyed heightening the dramatic irony of his quest: today it's a cinematic cliché.

"If she lived, doubtless we must have been sometimes in search of each other, at the very same moment, through the mighty labyrinths of London; perhaps even within a few feet of each other — a barrier no wider, in a London street, often amounting in the end to a separation for eternity."[7]

Ann, like his sister Elizabeth, became transfigured into a mythic Romantic figure. "Her cough which grieved me when I parted with her," wrote De Quincey, "is now my consolation."[8] Dead, defiled innocence was evidently more touching than the more complex and hurtful memory of Ann's continuing struggle for survival. Yet, though she was tidied away into a crystal of experience, De Quincey was plagued with flashes of regret for the rest of his life.

Exhausted and ill, Thomas gave in. He returned to Chester for a reconciliation with the family in March 1803, carrying with him the sad blast of experiences which had taken him far beyond his seventeen and a half years. The family would never stifle him again.

He was sent to a cottage in Everton to recover alone while his mother and guardians worried over the future plans of the young delinquent. During this period of inactivity Thomas kept an impressively detailed diary. Like those of most teenagers', Thomas' diary was kept most faithfully when he was depressed and lethargic: he had acres of time to cram into a page. The only significant change was the first detail of his sex life, albeit a disgusted and tired reference. "Go to the same fat whore's as I was at last time; give her 1s. and a cambrick pocket hand-kerchief," he noted glumly, "go home miserable."[9]

When he was not purging his body of desire, Thomas read Gothic novels, wrote ineffectual poetry, made notes on literary theory and dreamed of meeting Wordsworth. "My imagination flies, like Noah's dove, from the ark of my mind," wrote Thomas, "and finds no place on which to rest the sole of her foot except Coleridge — Wordsworth and Southey."[10]

After spending so long trying to establish "the intimate connection, which exists between the body and mind," (no doubt frustrated by his awakening sexuality) Thomas finally decided to put thought into action. He began to compose a letter to his idol on May 11th.

The following fortnight was spent in revisions, and the drafts in Thomas' diary show how he laboured to strike an appropriate tone. The mail-order formality of "I take this method of requesting . . ." was scrapped in favour of the more direct and compelling "To most men what I am going to say would seem strange." He wanted attention and his theatrical, intense letter which invested Wordsworth with all the qualities he felt he lacked himself was the essay of a committed acolyte. Wordsworth had won his most faithful fan. Throughout the letter Thomas is insistent in his desire for friendship, an insistence that was to sour his later relations with the poet.

". . . you will never find any one more zealously attached to you — more full of admiration for your mental excellence and of reverential love for your moral character — more ready . . . to sacrifice even his life — whenever it could have a chance of promoting your interest and happiness — than he who now bends the knee before you. And I will add that, to no man on earth except yourself and *one* other (a friend of your's), would I thus lowly and suppliantly prostrate myself."[11]

The passion and urgency must have moved the thirty-three-year-old Wordsworth, who was not yet famous and could not enjoy the luxury of scorning admirers. But the boy needed to be treated carefully. The burden of glory and hopes he had showered on the poet smacked of dangerous abandonment and despite the edge of pride in Thomas' letter, a careless word from Wordsworth would mortify the boy. The reply was a lesson in tact.

Wordsworth wrote within two days, and although "kindly disposed" toward Thomas, he moved gently: "My friendship it is not in my power to give: this is a gift which no man can make, it is not in our power: a sound and healthy friendship is the growth of time and circumstance."[12] He invited Thomas to Grasmere and, thinking he had been too brisk, added a long characteristic postscript saying he would like to see his admirer.

Oddly enough, the friendship bowled along quickly. After two letters Wordsworth's initial wisdom was cast aside and he signed himself "your very affectionate friend." Thomas' testimony that he had been "uplifted and purified" by his writings hit the most tremulous nerve in the conceited poet's body. The teacher reacted automatically to his pupil.

"Such facts as you have communicated to me," he wrote, "are an abundant recompense for all the labours and pains which the profession of poetry requires."[13]

Even if Wordsworth started, "I do not mean to preach . . ." he naturally did. The didactic urge was irresistible.

In Everton Thomas languished in "Chattertonian melancholia" and suffered a stomach complaint souvenir from his recent ordeal. He began to keep a close note of his health, and even detailed how many cups of tea he drank each day. The habit served him well in the coming years of opium addiction when he recorded dosage of laudanum and fretted over more debilitating illness.

Speculation on his own character followed Proustian threads and revealed that Thomas' sensibility had not been blunted by city deprivation. If anything, it demanded a tighter rein than ever before.

"My hopes and fears are alternately raised and quelled by the minutest — the most trivial circumstances — by the slightest words. Witness the dismay I used to feel on the approach of the holidays . . . if any person called it a long time until they would arrive or vice versa; tho' all along, I was fully sensible that the interval was not one moment lengthened by anything they could say. Witness too the *moideration* in which I leave Mrs. W if anything is said less flattering than on a preceding day: though, all the while, I am fully conscious that she does not regard me more or less on one day yn on another."[14]

Analysis was his forte, for he loved the mental discipline of worrying out distinctions. Although he was one of the earliest admirers of Wordsworth and had a keen critic's eye, the basic temperamental difference between himself and the poet of spirit was to forever separate them.

In December 1803 Thomas arrived at Oxford and rounded up his undergraduate friends to suggest a suitable college. His mother and guardians had simply packed him off with a £100 a year allowance — getting in was Thomas' problem. He settled for Christ Church and was interviewed by the surprised Dean, Dr. Cyril Jackson, who told him that there was not a dog kennel untenanted and, moreover, that he should have given a year's notice of his intentions. Despite the setback Thomas found secluded rooms in the humbler surroundings of Worcester.

Fellow students left him unimpressed with their racy lives of cock fighting, boxing, coursing and drinking. Anyway, it was well that he disapproved because he could not afford to join them. He remained aloof and solitary in the cherished knowledge of his secret correspondence with Wordsworth.

"In short, up to 1820, the name Wordsworth was trampled under foot; from 1820 to 1830, it was militant; from 1830 to 1835, it has been triumphant. In 1803 when I entered Oxford, that name was absolutely unknown . . ."[15]

Thomas was secure in his superiority over the "drinking, rattling set whose conversation was juvenile, commonplace and quite unintellectual," and, consequently, he withdrew from social life, read avidly and spent all his money on books. Lectures were as unsatisfying as society. He preferred to make his own digests of books rather than listen to someone else's, and so he skipped lectures whenever possible. It was the mark of a bright, impatient student; well-trodden paths through academia were for the timid and narrow. Thomas was neither. As for his tutor, Thomas met him just once in the early years, and then only by accident while crossing a quadrangle.

Once again time and experience seemed out of joint for the arrogant freshman. He felt he knew too much, and in some ways it was true.

"There was one reason why I sought solitude at that early age, and sought it in morbid excess, which must naturally have conferred upon my character some degree of that interest which belongs to all extremes. My eye had been couched into a secondary power of vision, by misery, by solitude, by sympathy with life in all its modes, by experiences too early won, and by the sense of danger critically escaped."[16]

Thomas' threadbare clothes led to a warning about his appearance from a senior college member, but the passion for book buying always came between Thomas and his desire to look unexceptional. He veered further away from set texts and with unerring taste picked up the then unknown works of Robert Southey and Walter Savage Landor. A vast, self-imposed curriculum of ancient and modern philosophy, and European literature left Thomas with little time for sleep. The regime was followed vigorously until he suffered a physical breakdown.

German studies were resumed with tuition from a fellow student until Thomas felt he was sufficiently fluent to cope with Kant's mighty treatise, the Critique of Pure Reason. But within six weeks he found that Kant's philosophy "destroys by wholesale, and substitutes nothing."[17] The dismay is understandable. Thomas probably expected a coherent argument which would bolster his own conditioned religious beliefs. Instead, he found a dry document preoccupied with splitting epistemological hairs. Despite this faltering first aquaintance, De Quincey and Coleridge can jointly lay claim to the introduction of the Kantian system to Britain. The former began his mission in The Westmorland Gazette when, as Editor, he promised to throw "the whole Danube of the profound German intellect into a channel accessible to English readers."[18] Even though the two essays that appeared in the Gazette could hardly be said to have burst the banks of the river of German knowledge before Westmorland readers, they were no small achievement for a provincial Editor. De Quincey never kept his full promise but he did produce enlightened essays arguing the superiority of a priori deduction over empirical reasoning.

The only interesting feature of Oxford life outside studies was a peculiar digression — a courtroom drama with special interest for Thomas. He knew the leading lady.

The case revolved around a certain Mrs. Lee and the question of whether she was abducted at gunpoint as the potential rape victim of two Oxford students and brothers, or whether she eloped with them. Mrs. Lee had caught Thomas' attention some years earlier when, at a dinner at Greenhay, her atheistic beliefs had put Mrs. De Quincey into a hysterical fit.

Thomas found a seat in the courtroom after jostling through the excited crowds queuing in the rain for a glimpse of the protagonists. After the reading of letters, which a local paper thought too indecent to publish, and cross-examination of the wronged lady, Mrs. Lee was finally trapped by her atheism. Her evidence under oath was rendered invalid. The brothers got off with a reprimand, and Mrs. Lee escaped in a carriage jeered by a mob.

The early interest in the theatre of court is significant. It marked the beginning of a fascination for the unravelling of human drama within the confines of Justice. It was an unrivalled spectacle of exposure.

As Editor of The Westmorland Gazette, De Quincey was to cram the pages of his newspaper with skilfully reworked trial reports, which not only offered excellent titillation, but aimed to serve a more solemn purpose — the moral education of readers. However, in De Quincey's day there were no restrictions on court reporting and the elegant precursor of today's 'sizzling schoolgirl' was born. Nineteenth century journalists were keen to thrill readers with brisk pen-portraits, and so the victim in a sex case could easily find herself as "a very pretty interesting English girl, of 19 years of age, and apparently extremely fascinating in her manners and address."[19] Evidently, the enthusiasm for type-casting had a long way to go before it stooped to self-parody. While De Quincey enjoyed juggling the complexities of evidence, his readers found simpler sources of pleasure. Explicit details of horrendous murders were popular, and even the Editor exhibited a rich taste in the macabre which foreshadowed his humorous and delightfully discursive essay, On Murder Considered as One of the Fine Arts, in 1827.

Thomas' Oxford depression remained unrelieved. News of Pink's running away to sea naturally caused a flood of guilt about how far his own example may have inspired the fourteen-year-old. In a second attempt to flee the floggings he endured at school, Pink became a cabin boy on a privateer before transferring to a whaler bound for the South Seas. Spectacular adventures followed: capture by pirates who press-ganged him to navigate their marauding ship after massacring his crewmates; the storming of Monte Video in 1807 and capture by the Danes at the battle of Copenhagen.

In his anguish, Thomas now broke a two year silence in his correspondence with Wordsworth, and for the first time admitted someone into his sanctuary of isolation and cell of fears. Thomas revealed his grief and regret over the loss of his brother, he apologised for the lack of contact and excused himself on the grounds of an "unconfirmed pulmonary consumption."

Despite the inherent difficulties of resuming correspondence after such a long delay, Thomas could be assured of a sympathetic response. His disdain for university life must have been shared by Wordsworth, and the wanderings in Wales bore a marked resemblance to the poet's own travels in France in the 1790's when he was evading family plans for him to enter the church. The student and his adopted father-confessor had mutual ground, or at least parallel experience. They still had to meet.

Thomas may have opened his heart to Wordsworth in that letter of April 5th 1806, but he carefully neglected to mention his most exciting discovery during the previous two years —opium.

Book buying had reached such a pitch that Thomas visited the money lender Dell in London in Autumn 1804 and borrowed £250 at the rate of 17½ per cent . While in the city, he was plagued by an excruciating toothache and a college friend innocently suggested opium, well-known as a panacea and painkiller. On a dull, wet Sunday afternoon Thomas entered a druggist's and bought the first tincture. It was an unremarkable event. The drug was easily available and in common use. Its effect was rather more memorable.

"But I took it: — and in an hour, oh! heavens! what a revulsion! what a resurrection, from its lowest depths, of the inner spirit! what an apocalypse of the world within me! That my pains had vanished was now a trifle in my eyes; — this negative effect was swallowed up in the immensity of those positive effects which had suddenly opened before me, in the abyss of divine enjoyment thus suddenly revealed. Here was a panacea . . . for all human woes; here was the secret of happiness, about which philosophers had disputed for so many ages, at once discovered; happiness might now be bought for a penny, and carried in the waistcoat-pocket; portable ecstasies might be had corked up in a pint-bottle; and peace of mind could be sent down by the mail."[20]

Chapter Three

Greeting the Dark Interpreter

". . . the Dark Interpreter does his work, revealing the worlds of pain and agony and woe possible to man — possible even to the innocent spirit of a child."

Thomas De Quincey, Suspira De Profundis.

There was nothing special about De Quincey's discovery. Oppressed mill workers in Lancashire took opium to kill drudgery, and factory wives dosed their babies to keep them drowsy while left unattended. Use was widespread: in one Lancashire town there were 1,600 regular buyers of the opium-based potion Godfrey's Syrup, and druggists often lined up tinctures on the counter, ready for the evening rush. Opium was, indeed, the opium of the people. There was nothing fanciful about the drug to cotton workers who wanted to smother the screaming of miserable children. They just reached for the bottle when the bleating or despair became unbearable.

In 1830 Britain imported 22,000lbs of opium to keep both doctors and workers happy — but there was also a third demand. Despite its common use, opium retained an aura of excitement and eroticism among the intelligentsia, who were seduced by the promise of an Arabian ambrosia. De Quincey may have first taken it as a pain-killer, but the reason soon became an excuse. Under the influence of opium he became elated, a possessor of wisdom who experienced the subconscious remote control of his dreams and who could steer away from unpleasant sequences. The pilot's seat felt very nice indeed. Things changed when he became a passenger.

Opium is the dried juice of the poppy. The drug is obtained by incising the seed-heads and collecting and drying the exuded juice. The milky substance coagulates, turns brown when exposed to air and is rolled into small cakes like putty. It contains many alkaloids, the most important being morphine. The interaction of the alkaloids creates the narcotic effect and gives an inner glow of peace and power. No wonder, then, that opium became such a popular cure-all for rheumatism, consumption, chest problems, cholera, syphilis and anything else in the medical dictionary. Paradoxically, it was also sold as a constipation cure. This was the biggest myth of all because the first physical effects of addiction hit the alimentary canal, as Coleridge and De Quincey would have testified: they both suffered from chronic constipation throughout their adult lives. Worse still, opium usually suppressed symptoms rather than cured ailments.

De Quincey's first experience of opium was in the form of a tincture known as laudanum. This solution of opium in alcohol was easily bought at any druggist. Ways of measuring a dose were rough but a small teaspoon held about 100 drops (four grains of opium). By 1816 De Quincey's daily intake was 8,000 drops: heavy, but certainly not suicidal. Today, intravenous injections of morphine and heroin have narrowed the bridge between addiction and death, giving a serious junkie about two years' grace. In De Quincey's day the process was much slower because the opium was taken orally; in fact, a 19th century addict could live a long and fruitful life, and die naturally of something totally unrelated to the drug.

The Black Drop was a Lake District speciality which secured Coleridge's addiction during the winter of 1800. Found exclusively in North Lancashire and Westmorland, this solution of opium in vegetable acids was about twice the strength of normal laudanum. Three Quaker business rivals each claimed the original recipe. John Airey Braithwaite (1758-1810), a surgeon, marketed The Lancashire Genuine Black Drop[1] as having all the desirable effects of opium, but without the sickness and headaches that came to be associated with laudanum. When he died, the recipe passed into the hands of his sister Margaret who ran an ironmongery in Yard 25 at Kirkland, in Kendal, with her brother. Secrecy and Macbeth were the key to her publicity, for tales spread of how the brew was simmered for a month and stirred at night by masked assistants. The unsocial hours paid well. The stuff was sold at the astonishing price of eleven shillings for four ounces and made the family a fortune. Such was the fuss that the recipe was said to have been finally sold at public auction. In the early 1800's two other Quakers set up in opposition to the Braithwaites: Ann Todd mixed her potion in a yard behind the Commercial Inn at Kendal and charged only 1/6d, while Hannah Backhouse advertised her Black Drop in The Westmorland Gazette. De Quincey could hardly have avoided the hard sell.

It was all too easy for De Quincey to become an addict, and the psychological dependence upon an available means of escape was the first stage. De Quincey disliked physical pain and would avoid or postpone it at any cost. For example, he endured the pain of a rotten tooth for weeks rather than submit himself to the brief, intense hurt of extraction. In the same way that Proust forever feared the death of things and people he loved, De Quincey feared his own judgement; each writer was haunted by his own personal preoccupation. Procrastination kept the world at bay from De Quincey, but in turn it welcomed opium. Family guilt, depression, solitude and debts also smoothed the road to addiction.

"I hanker too much after a state of happiness, both for myself and others; I cannot face a misery, whether my own or not, with an eye of sufficient firmness, and am little capable of encountering present pain for the sake of any revisionary benefit."[2]

The building up of the body's tolerance to opium means that increasingly frequent and larger doses are needed until eventually the body's chemistry changes. Under this saturation the body begins to crave the drug. The physical effects of giving up actually become worse than continuing the dosage and include hyperacidity, gastritis, heavy sweating, sleeplessness and a sense of hideous oppression. Addiction is like eating for subsistence —gastronomic delight disappears. In De Quincey's case, addiction started around 1813, a few years before his Editorship of The Westmorland Gazette; but in the meantime the honeymoon was a glorious, illicit feast.

During 1805 De Quincey's pattern of drug taking certainly did not tend towards solitude. Quite the contrary. He actively sought company and external stimulants in London on his drug-infused sorties. In his Confessions, De Quincey begs lenient judgement: "I was a hard student, and at severe studies for all the rest of my time; and certainly I had a right occasionally to relaxations as well as other people."[3] Sudden excesses were not his style; he preferred to anticipate and plan outings which would exact fine peaks of pleasure.

"The late Duke of Norfolk used to say, 'Next Monday, wind and weather permitting, I purpose to be drunk'; and in like manner I used to fix beforehand how often within a given time, when, and with what accessory circumstances of festal joy, I would commit a debauch of opium."[4]

Every three weeks, on a Tuesday or Saturday night, he headed for the King's Theatre to hear the famous contralto Josephina Grassini. He was awash with sensation as he trembled in the cheap seats waiting for his idol, surrounded by Italian opera enthusiasts, whose melodic, incomprehensible tongue swirled inside his head. De Quincey's communal experience of the concert must have been similar to a hippy rock festival of the 1960's as the drug honed the apex of joy to a lingering agony.

"Thrilling was the pleasure with which almost always I heard this angelic Grassini. Shivering with expectation I sat, when the time grew near for her golden epiphany; shivering I rose from my seat, incapable of rest, when that heavenly and harp-like voice sang its own victorious welcome threttanelo —threttanelo. The choruses were divine to hear; and, when Grassini appeared in some interlude, as she often did, and poured forth her passionate soul as Andromache at the tomb of Hector, etc., I question whether any Turk, of all that ever entered the paradise of opium-eaters, can have had half the pleasure I had."[5]

His power of dreaming, cultivated through his childhood, combined with the drug to recreate the music in a rolling, visual frieze of his past life. It was a sublime experience of cinema and opera. Music was not just a component of such drug joys; in later years it became the primary strength of his conversation and prose when he literally composed passages as if they were intricate fugues. De Quincey had discovered how external influences, such as the lofty ballroom at Shrewsbury, altered his reveries, but now opium multiplied their effects.

"It is all but inconceivable to men of unyielding and callous sensibilities," wrote De Quincey, "how profoundly others find their reveries modified and overruled by the external character of the immediate scene around them."[6]

This note prefigures Proust, whose four critical memories of A La Recherche Du Temps Perdu were stirred by small physical events. Tripping on a pavement took Marcel back to the Baptistry of St. Mark in Venice, and the feel of a napkin on his lips at a party recalled the roughness of a towel after a swim at Balbec. By comparison, De Quincey seemed to need excessive stimulation, but this was partly because he was far more inhibited about his recollections. For De Quincey, life could be a game of tag between reality and fantasy as in those childhood days of self-imposed terror.

"Perhaps you are aware of that power in the eye of many children by which in darkness they project a vast theatre of phantasmagorical figures moving forwards or backwards between their bed-curtains and the chamber walls. In some children this power is semi-voluntary —they can control or perhaps suspend the shows; but in others it is altogether automatic."[7]

We can guess that De Quincey was a weak director in a company of tyrant actors. In a similar fashion, Proust found the magic lantern image of Golo the horseman charming, but he still felt qualms at the mystery of the whole room transformed into a stage with Golo galloping across curtains, doors and into make-believe shadow castles. Both writers were disturbed by the exercise of mental control, or perhaps the lack of it.

Although De Quincey enjoyed drugs in company, there were rules to his essentially private experience. The people were strangers, and when he wandered the city streets, he existed in a capsule, detached from all he surveyed like a visiting deity. On Saturday nights he occasionally haunted London markets and watched and listened to the families spending their wages. "Gradually," he remembered, "I became familiar with their wishes, their difficulties and their opinions."[8] De Quincey in his drugged-up dreamworld would eavesdrop and even give gratuitous advice to the surprised parties before resuming the floating tour of his kingdom. This uninvited consumer service had none of the contempt of the usual Oxford slumming. De Quincey possessed a genuine empathy for those inhabiting the spectacle. His hopes rose and fell with the poor because he knew exactly what it felt like to live on the breadline; although, of course, any depression at the sights was quickly cured by an extra dose of laudanum. He was flirting with the shadows of his own recent past, and somewhere among the strangely orchestrated cast was Ann of Oxford Street.

"For all this, however I paid a heavy price in distant years, when the human face tyrannised over my dreams, and the perplexities of my steps in London came back and haunted my sleep, with the feeling of perplexities, moral or intellectual, that brought confusion to the reason, that brought anguish and remorse to the conscience."[9]

As early as the summer of 1805 family doctors, ignorant of his drug habit, checked De Quincey's symptoms of sweating, poor breathing and weakness, and diagnosed consumption. Reports of opium's ill-effects on Eastern addicts were becoming common knowledge but De Quincey ignored them; as a 'consumptive' he was as good as dead anyway. This diagnosis finally confirmed his pessimistic view of his own health and probably came as a relief.

De Quincey made his first trip to the Lake District on his mission to meet Wordsworth the same year, but his nerve failed him. In 1806 he tried again to no avail. He even got as far as seeing his idol's cottage, but felt too embarrassed and unworthy to reveal himself. Like most people threatened with the reality of meeting their hero, he was tongue-tied. He was so determined to make a good impression that it was pride, not cowardice, that forced a retreat. De Quincey scuttled back to a small inn at Coniston and, three days after his twenty-first birthday on August 18th, he busied himself listing the "constituents of Happiness".

The twelve points included: a capacity for thinking; an interest in all human life; a fixed residence in an area of natural beauty; an interchange of solitude and society; books; a great intellectual project; health and vigour; contemplation; freedom from material worries; the education of a child and a physical appearance which was "tolerably respectable." This final clause stemmed from De Quincey's worry over his diminutive size. He longed hopelessly to be "on a level with the persons of men generally," and thought this apparent defect could be offset by acquiring a "high literary fame". His lack of physical stature was noticed by others: Dorothy Wordsworth thought him "very diminutive in person, which, to strangers makes him appear insignificant," and even Southey called him "little Mr. De Quincey" and wrote "I wish he were not so little". But most people, especially women, found him dapper, pretty and a sparkling conversationalist. De Quincey never lost sight of his goals and worked implacably towards achievement. On balance he was fairly successful though, of course, he never grew much over five foot four.

Back at college in Spring 1807, De Quincey heard that Coleridge and Wordsworth were in London. A month after the news, he went to the city only to find they had already left. He had missed the boat again. Even before De Quincey's failed Lake District excursions, Wordsworth's curiosity was killing him. "I cannot bear the thought that you should be in the North and I not see you," he wrote to his mystery admirer.[10]

While staying with his mother at Bristol during the summer vacation, De Quincey was told that Coleridge was at Nether Stowey, less than a day's ride away. He went in search and eventually met Coleridge riding down Main Street, at Bridgewater.

". . . his person was broad and full, and tended even to

corpulence; his complexion was fair, though not what painters technically style fair, because it was associated with black hair; his eyes were large, and soft in their expression; and it was from the peculiar appearance of haze or dreaminess which mixed with their light that I recognised my object. This was Coleridge."[11]

As ever, the poet offered friendship easily and the welcome was warm. In a drawing room over drinks, Coleridge gave De Quincey a glittering display; it was not a conversation but a monologue. He talked for three hours and left his admirer spellbound. The maze of erudition, aphorisms and illustrative digressions lost the common herd, but not De Quincey.

"Coleridge, to many people, and often I have heard the complaint, seemed to wander; and he seemed then to wander most when, in fact, his resistance to the wandering instinct was greatest — viz., when the compass and huge circuit, by which his illustrations moved, travelled farthest into remote regions before they began to revolve. Long before this coming round commenced, most people had lost him, and naturally enough supposed that he had lost himself."[12]

At sunset De Quincey and Coleridge shared a walk during which the younger made a tentative reference about opium. He had reason to regret it for Coleridge seized the opportunity to express his horror at the "hideous bondage" of the drug. The thirty-seven-year-old poet was preoccupied. He had a wife and three children, had recently returned from Malta after a vain bid to strengthen his health and needed money badly. He was suffering withdrawal symptoms from opium and the strain was showing in his marriage. Yet, despite the problems, Coleridge satisfied expectations and held court at dinner, resigned to the misunderstanding and confusion of many of those who listened. The sharp young De Quincey had a reservation, and was perhaps too harsh on his idol: "With the riches of El Dorado lying about him, he would condescend to filch a handful of gold from any man whose purse he fancied."[13] Coleridge was notoriously indiscreet when in pursuit of a fugitive theory — attribution just got trampled in the dash for capture. In more kindly vein, Lord Egmont gently moved: "He talks like an angel, and does nothing at all."

The autumn of 1807 found De Quincey on close terms with the Coleridge family at Bristol, and "the greatest man that has ever appeared" aghast with worry over a series of lectures for the Royal Institution. Through Joseph Cottle, the original publisher of the Lyrical Ballads, De Quincey anonymously gave £300, almost a quarter of his patrimony, to Coleridge. It was a generous, if reckless gift and a few subtle hints from Cottle secured De Quincey's favour. With Coleridge tied to London by his lecture schedule, De Quincey stepped into the breach again. He escorted Mrs. Coleridge with her children Sara, Derwent and Hartley on their visit to Wordsworth at Grasmere and Southey at Greta Hall, Keswick. The family entrance was an ideal mode of introduction to his hero because he finally had the perfect excuse to turn up on his doorstep.

They arrived in Ambleside in the afternoon of November 4th. But at the summit of White Moss at 4 p.m. De Quincey and the children became so impatient that they climbed off the chaise to run the rest of the way down towards Grasmere. As the sound of wheels faded behind them, they turned a corner and saw Town End with two yew trees breaking the white glare of its walls. Only Hartley Coleridge, who swept up to the garden gate, prevented the rising panic of recognition from the year before. De Quincey was ten yards away from the front door when Wordsworth appeared, strode up and shook his hand. The moment was lost as the chaise arrived outside, and the poet went to greet Mrs. Coleridge. With the long anticipated catastrophe averted, De Quincey entered the house agog. He had been accepted without question.

As far as gods go, Wordsworth was a mixed bag in terms of physical beauty. This was probably a relief to the short De Quincey, who concluded with some satisfaction: "He was, upon the whole, not a well-made man." The poet had a long face with a fine and sombre complexion like that of a Spanish monk. His nose was large and arched, which probably contributed to the sheep-like impression that so reminded De Quincey of Milton. He had eyes which were neither bright, lustrous nor piercing, but which after a hard day's walk could assume a spiritual mien. His forehead was "remarkable for its breadth and expansive development" but it was certainly not lofty. The reality and the fantasy clashed; if Wordsworth's head was hardly an example of the classical expectation of genius, then worse was to come.

In a particularly testy passage of his Recollections of the Lake Poets, De Quincey frittered over 600 words on the relative merits and deficiencies of Wordsworth's legs — possibly because they were longer than his own. The limbs in question were stocky models of practicality not elegant decoration, which, as De Quincey mused, had carried their owner over 175,000 miles. Even so, he wrote: "Wordsworth was of a good height (five feet ten), and not a slender man; on the contrary, by the side of Southey, his limbs looked thick, almost in a disproportionate degree. But the total effect of Wordsworth's person was always worse in a state of motion."[14]

Dorothy Wordsworth fared a little better in De Quincey's reflections. She was unlike any woman he had ever encountered, and more akin to a wild poppy than an English rose. "Rarely, in a woman of English birth, had I seen a more determinate gipsy tan," noted De Quincey. Dorothy's manner was so ardent that it sadly demanded checking if she was to maintain the standard of decorum expected of her sex in the 1800's. But on occasion her natural spirit broke convention and, although her voice faltered, the passion was true.

"Even her very utterances and enunciation often suffered in point of clearness and steadiness, from the agitation of her excessive organic sensibility. At times, the self-counteraction and self-baffling of her feelings caused her to stammer . . ."[15]

Dorothy's intellectual prowess and sensitivity were apparently countered by her lack of deportment, for De Quincey thought her stooping walk gave her a graceless and "unsexual" appearance. It was difficult for him to reconcile such contrasting features, but he remained charmed, partly because the sisterly relationship was so close to him. The shared experience of Dorothy and William is described by an obvious marital metaphor when De Quincey says that Dorothy "engrafted, with her delicate female touch, those graces upon the ruder growths of his nature, which have since clothed the forest of his genius with a foliage corresponding in loveliness and beauty to the strength of its boughs and the massiness of its trunk."[16]

It was a usurpation of Mrs. Wordsworth's role. Mary remained in the shadows and was hampered by the traditional virtues of sweetness and courtesy, but moreover by her lack of experience and mental vigour. "She had seen nothing of high life," wrote De Quincey dismissively, "for she had seen little of any."[17]

De Quincey was always sceptical about Wordsworth's capacity for self-surrender. The poet was certainly not a man to humour feminine caprice, and his austerity seemed to deny the devotion of courtship at every turn. The crazy affair with Annette Vallon in France, and the memory of vowing to return home to take holy orders when his lover was two months pregnant, must have made his cheeks burn. It was Wordsworth's one loss of control. Yet despite the responding check on emotions, De Quincey, who never knew of his hero's secret affair, conceded: "Few people have lived on such terms of entire harmony and affection, as he lived with the woman of his final choice."[18]

The Wordsworth household set little store on luxuries outside the basic creature comforts. This combination of high-brow aspirations and plain living must have confused De Quincey, who was more used to his mother's society round in Bath. On the morning after his arrival he found Dorothy preparing breakfast and a common kettle whistling over the fire. Meal over, De Quincey joined sister and brother for a six mile walk in the rain around Rydal and Grasmere. It was a dream come true.

The next day they took a ride north on the back of a cart and after a brief tour followed Mrs. Coleridge who was visiting Southey at Great Hall, near Keswick. De Quincey was surprised by two things: firstly, the bizarre garb of Southey, who wore a jacket and pantaloons and looked like a "Tyrolese mountainer;" and secondly, the tone of a political conversation between the two poets. The gist of the upset was a joke about deporting the royal family to Australia — sheer heresy to the ears of a staunch young Tory. De Quincey knew little about the riptide of enthusiasm the two men had shared in the early days of the French Revolution, so the jest came as a shock. Even so, he buried his doubts and smiled politely.

By November 14th De Quincey was back in Oxford trying to keep term, and probably assimilating his new position as a friend of Wordsworth. Despite his apparent acceptance, it was not all he had hoped for. He was a great success with the Wordsworth children and the womenfolk, less with the poet himself. The following year, Sara Hutchinson described De Quincey as "a good tempered amiable creature and uncommonly clever and an excellent scholar," but it was not the judgement he wanted. The words should have come from the mouth of Wordsworth. It is telling that from De Quincey's return to Oxford, Dorothy became his main confidant, not her brother. She offered an intimacy that William was unable to give and could nurture the student's brittle ego. This situation was the root of what was to become a long-standing problem, but for the moment De Quincey was content.

Early in 1808 Coleridge was in a critical state, wallowing uncomfortably above the offices of the Courier in the Strand with only the clatter of noisy presses and stamp of printers' feet to fill his reveries. From four flights up, Coleridge would appear "picturesquely enveloped in nightcaps, surmounted by handkerchiefs,"[19] and scream down the stairwell for his servant Mrs. Brainbridge. The din from the newspaper offices often drowned his pleas, and Coleridge slumped back on his bed drained. De Quincey heard of his plight and became his nurse. For a couple of months he ran errands, found him books, and researched bits for his dwindling lecture dates at the Royal Institution. If De Quincey had had the wit to look he would have seen the results of Coleridge's fading attempts to go cold turkey. The opium was no longer the problem; it was the denial of the body's need that was now crippling the poet. Ironically, the patient was fighting not to take the drug while the nurse happily dosed up.

Eventually Oxford called him to heel. He returned to college in March with little course work under his belt and the prospect of exams in the early summer. The mere thought of this imminent catastrophy was enough to bring him down with nervous exhaustion although, of course, the situation was in part of his own making. He deceived himself. De Quincey did not just suddenly find himself prostrate before the lion again, he actually scoured the jungle to offer himself as sacrifice.

". . . finding the whole university on tiptoe for the approaching prize-fighting and myself in a state of palsy as to any power of exertion, I felt very much as in dreams which I recollect where I have been chased by a lion and spellbound from even attempting to escape."[20]

He told Dorothy, perhaps with the glee of the irredeemably depressed, that he would have to plough through thirty Greek tragedies in one week. Sleep was lost in worry, and although De Quincey spent eighteen hours a day studying, little seemed to stick. His brain was like a pumping station flushing information through his paralysed mind. A vast range of subjects, and the fact that each student picked his own books and topics, added extra piquancy to his panic. The memory of the Rev. Hall and his dreaded rote tests must have peered maliciously over his shoulder, as choice degenerated into random fragments grasped in fear. This appetite for the terror of impossible deadlines would be put on trial again only once before De Quincey's Editorship of the Gazette.

On Saturday May 14th De Quincey was tested in Latin and fared so well that an examiner said that the nervous, little student was "the cleverest man" he had ever met. But De Quincey failed to show on the Monday for the Greek exam. He never went back. He fled to London, probably in the misplaced fear of disappointing his college in the academic games.

His suspicions about the whole exam system were revealed in a letter to Dorothy: "The motives to all this labour are besides inadequate; for the difference between success and non-success are the being placarded on all the college walls as the Illustrious . . . as the Praiseworthy . . . or . . . the not being placarded at all . . ."[21] He mimicked Wordsworth in his disdain, but there is a false note. De Quincey may well have become disillusioned after all his pains, but he was an achiever who needed the appreciation of others. This time he dropped out, not in defiance, but from genuine fear of failure.

He spent the summer in London and visited Everton before taking up Dorothy's invitation to Grasmere. When he arrived at the Wordsworths' new home, Allan Bank, he found it packed with people and ideas. Coleridge and his family, Mary Wordsworth and her sister Sara Hutchinson were all there, bringing the total to fifteen, including Wordsworth's newborn Catherine. William was buried in politics while Coleridge was fretting to Sara Hutchinson, the object of his vain passion, over a new periodical called The Friend. De Quincey reeled with the excitement of it all and became everyone's assistant.

In time-honoured tradition Coleridge made things as difficult as possible for himself, and instead of having The Friend printed in Kendal, he chose Penrith, twenty-eight miles away with the dreadfully steep Kirkstone Pass in between. De Quincey later admitted that the poet made decisions with "downright crazy disregard"[22] for common sense, but at the time he suggested setting up a press in Grasmere to print "immaculate editions" of the classics as well as Coleridge's literary magazine. The two dreamers really were birds of a feather. The content of The Friend was as uncompromising as its chosen form of production. Little effort was made to woo the readership and in later years De Quincey went so far as to condemn the subjects as "chosen obstinately in defiance of the popular taste."[23] After twenty-nine issues The Friend had made few. Coleridge missed deadlines and the printer went bankrupt. The whole affair was delightfully whimsical; for example, De Quincey, as circulation manager, became the largest single subscriber and he often sent out copies unordered. With two such captains of finance at the helm it was surprising that The Friend did not sink as soon as it came proudly off the slipway. It defied logic and floated uneasily. Coleridge sometimes wrote nothing for weeks and then polished off a whole issue in two days, dictating all the while to Sara Hutchinson. She was probably close to mutiny by the end of his staccato voyage into publishing, and she left Allan Bank in February 1810, tired of his unpredictable habits and inevitable drug taking. The Wordsworths bit their tongues. The temptation to say 'I told you so' must have been irresistible as they sat back and saw Coleridge destroy another of his own plans. Dorothy only wished that he had been forced to print locally and so have no excuse for failure.

"If he had been able to stay quietly here," she wrote to De Quincey, "the trial would have been a fair one — and should he have failed, in future one could never, in case of any other scheme, be vexed with hopes and fears."[24]

The comment is revealing because it shows how close De Quincey had become to the Wordsworth family. They trusted him enough to express doubts about their dear, if infuriating friend. The young man, so very eager to please, was a natural success with the children; he loved five-year-old John and unreservedly adored Catherine. For one with intellectual pretentions, De Quincey was in grave danger of becoming merely a pleasant house-guest. But Wordsworth soon found a new use for him.

Wordsworth had long been intrigued by politics. He had been stirred by the ideals of the French Revolution, and although his passion had survived The Terror, it had evaporated when Switzerland was invaded. His volte-face was the sort of thing that brought him out in patriotic sonnets. The latest interest was a long, convoluted row about the Peninsular War caused by the Convention of Cintra. This affair was misunderstood then, and is virtually forgotten now.

Under the Convention, French troops were evacuated from Portugal with their arms and booty and shipped home by the English. This may have been a neat logistic move but it insulted Portugal, England's ally. Wordsworth's moral indignation was whipped to a frenzy by the injustice and he busied himself with a pamphlet. De Quincey was then despatched to London to see the tome through the presses.

Proof reader to Wordsworth was a position of no mean responsibility. The political pamphlet may have been prose but it was a creative enterprise as close to Wordsworth's heart as his poems: to delegate anything to a third party was a wrench. But De Quincey already had a clear idea of the poet's stance on the controversy, and Coleridge had recognised his "old bachelor preciseness" in his dealings with the ill-fated Friend.

"As the subject of punctuation in prose was one to which I had never attended, and had of course settled no scheme of it in my mind," said Wordsworth loftily, "I departed that office to Mr. De Quincey."[25]

If De Quincey had known what he was in for, he might never have gone. As soon as he arrived in London the corrections started arriving daily. The pamphlet was a family affair with Wordsworth grinding out the copy and Coleridge doing the rewrites, but once in London the tract was out of their hands. De Quincey was the ideal scapegoat for the most minor of irritations, and with interest waning on the Convention, he was running the risk of delivering Wordsworth's stillborn child.

Letters arrived from Grasmere giving vague instructions on each of the instalments De Quincey received. He did his best revising, punctuating and phrasing, but his efforts did not satisfy either Wordsworth or Coleridge, possibly because he tried too hard. Wordsworth always wanted the last word on every tiny decision, and so the pamphlet lost its vital virtue, immediacy. Three months after De Quincey arrived in London, the pamphlet was completed on May 24th.

Wordsworth could only bring himself to give a grudging compliment to De Quincey for all his hard work. "The punctuation pleased me much; though there are here and there trifling errors in it," he wrote. "I think indeed your plan of punctuation admirable."[26] As usual he could not give without taking as well. Privately, De Quincey's precise punctuation was held responsible for the delay, and Southey and Coleridge unjustly said that it made the pamphlet unreadable. The exasperated editorial assistant was lucky to be ignorant of the harsh and unfair criticism that was flying about in Westmorland; he was already bruised by Wordsworth's snub on his own offer to bring the pamphlet up to date. The poet complained of headaches and sent inadequate briefs; he had no right to be peeved at De Quincey for his own shortcomings and complacency. It was De Quincey who was forced to take control after Wordsworth's loss of courage during a libel scare.

He even pushed through one suspect, yet trivial passage to prevent further print delays; an act which mortified the timid poet. The pamphlet was, as H. G. Wells might have said, not so much published as carried screaming into the street. There, it was soothed by a few favourable reviews before being silenced by universal oversight.

Wordsworth missed the punch of topicality, but anyway, his pamphlet said more about the universal than the particular. It was a trumpet for his conviction that national independence and liberty were the product of every human virtue working in harmony. This was a comment not just on war affecting the Iberian Peninsular, but every modern war. Wordsworth saw himself as a prophet of freedom and patriotism who asserted "the sanctity of principles and passions which are the natural birthright of man." [27] Stirring stuff. The pamphlet was reprinted in 1915 to bolster enthusiasm for the most modern war the world had ever seen. However, only the converted bothered to read it even then.

Wordsworth, resigned to the disappointment of his first venture into political journalism, wrote to Daniel Stuart, co-proprietor of the Courier. He absolved himself and damned De Quincey: "But it avails nothing to find fault, especially with me (who) has taken pains (according to the best of his judgement) to forward this business — that he has failed is too clear, and not without blame on his own part (being a man of great abilities and the best feelings, but, as I have found not fitted for smooth and speedy progress in business)."[28]

Back to the minor skirmishes of friendships, Coleridge, who was five months behind issuing the first Friend, gave a hypocritical flourish to Stuart by saying that De Quincey was "anxious yet dilatory, confused over accuracy, and at once systematic and labyrinthine." [29] He added that he was surprised that Wordsworth entrusted anything beyond correction of the proofs to De Quincey. It was a faithless lash because at the time De Quincey was also busy sending out prospectuses for Coleridge's overdue Friend.

Daniel Stuart may even have started the round of irritations and frictions about De Quincey's performance, since he, too, was offering editorial hints to speed the pamphlet on its way. He had been a friend to both Coleridge and Wordsworth since his days as Editor of the Morning Post, so it was natural for the trio to close ranks on the new boy. If De Quincey did cause any delays in publication, it was through excessive diligence, not laziness. He only wanted to do his hero justice and felt hurt at the cool reception to his Herculean endeavours.

During the same period De Quincey corresponded with the Wordsworth womenfolk, exchanging chat, gossip and family news. Above all, he loved to hear about the children. In London he bought them pictures and books, and he found a missing volume for their father's set of State Trials. But William never cared for books as material objects and remained unimpressed. "No applause ensued, not an atom of sympathy did I receive,"[30] wrote De Quincey, a man to whom appreciation was all.

The exposure to Wordsworth's family life prompted De Quincey's own nesting urge, and he decided to settle at Grasmere. While Dorothy wrote of all the preparations being made for his final move to his new home at Town End, De Quincey bought such wonders as a patent smoke dispenser to cure the smoky chimney at Allan Bank. He was well on his way to achieving his "constituents of Happiness," with the promise of solitude and society in the Wordsworth circle, and a home in an area of natural beauty. Next on his list was the education of a child, and De Quincey put in his bid for a pupil. He wanted Catherine to be his protégé.

"Mr. De Quincey has made us promise that he is to be her sole tutor," wrote Dorothy, "so we shall not dare to show her a letter in a book when she is old enough to have the wit to learn."[31]

In the meantime Dorothy planned all the furnishings of his home, and noted his affection for pink and white in bedrooms and hatred of bed hangings. The letters read like those of newly weds. Even De Quincey's sister Jane gave him a gentle nudge, asking whether that "beautiful and wild-hearted girl" ought to be consulted about his new cottage. Dorothy was hardly a girl. She was thirty-eight, nearly thirteen years De Quincey's senior;

but even so, marriage was not beyond the realms of possibility. Sara Hutchinson, too, joined in the welcoming party. "Your orchard," she wrote, "is the most beautiful spot on earth." Little did she know about his plan for radical pruning.

In London most of De Quincey's friends were absent, and he sought company in coffee houses. One of his more curious acquaintances was "Walking" Stewart, an eccentric philosopher who had explored most countries in Europe and Asia on foot, and wrote peculiar books like The Roll of a Tennis Ball through the Moral World. When he gave De Quincey a couple of works he urged him to bury them seven feet underground at Town End and at a cove under Helvellyn. They may still be there, in all their subversive glory. Stewart, the son of a linendraper, led a bizarre life and had been secretary to a native prince, the Narwaub of Arcot. He had a war wound in his head like a one inch dent and wandered about London in Armenian clothes. One of his favourite pastimes was to sit in St. James' Park "in trance-like reverie amongst the cows, inhaling their balmy breath and pursuing philosophic speculations." Wordsworth had met Stewart in Paris in 1792 and was captivated by his eloquence. De Quincey had first seen him in Bath in 1798 and now, after reading his works, had a chance for a closer look. He noted his conversation and theories, and used them later for a magazine article.

"I could not close my eyes to the many evidences which his writings and his conversation afforded of a true grandeur of mind, and of a calm spinosistic state of contemplative reverie. In fact, he was half crazy."[32]

Stewart badgered De Quincey to translate his volumes of philosophy into Latin to provide against the extinction of the English language. But most of his work died with him when in 1822 he was found in his Northumberland Street rooms with an empty bottle of laudanum at his side.

For months after the Cintra pamphlet's publication De Quincey lingered in London; Town End was ready in August, but the tenant did not arrive until October. Pink had turned up in Spring and tentatively exchanged letters with De Quincey, but it was not until September that he was reunited with the family at Westhay, in Somerset. This was one reason for Thomas' unwillingness to head north, but not the full story. In one of Coleridge's more affectionate letters to his wife, he remarked: "... between ourselves he is as great *a To-morrower* to the full as your poor husband."[33] It was true: De Quincey dithered. He was speculating on a trip to Greece, Turkey, Syria and Egypt, perhaps with a fleeting visit to Nubia thrown in for good measure. This idea, which could have been inspired by his chats with Stewart, faded quickly, perhaps because even De Quincey had doubts about his chances of survival on such a ridiculous, ambitious enterprise. He decided upon a quick trip to Spain as a consolation; however, Napoleon scotched those plans and De Quincey went to Town End. It was a much better idea altogether for a short-sighted, bookish creature who sipped laudanum and seemed unable to make up his mind. Yet for all his indecision, De Quincey was well on his way to achieving what he most wanted out of life only three years after establishing his goals. He could be deceptively consistent.

Chapter Four

For Better or Worse

> *"No man needs to search for paradox in this world of ours. Let him simply confine himself to the truth, and he will find paradox growing everywhere under his hands as rank as weeds."*
>
> *Thomas De Quincey, wks I, 199.*

The whole vale of Grasmere was excited at the prospect of De Quincey's arrival. The ceaseless delivery of crates heightened interest to an unprecedented pitch as villagers watched and speculated. Dorothy was dashing round the Lakes making the final preparations as she enlisted seamstresses to run up curtains, bought pots and pans in Kendal and commissioned £17 17s 8d worth of shelves from a Grasmere carpenter. Despite her good intentions, Dorothy underestimated De Quincey, and his mountain of books turned into an avalanche. Even after ten chests of books had arrived, some nineteen more were still expected. It was like the advance caravan of the world's most erudite potentate. The dales folk gossiped and agreed — Wordsworth was definitely low key compared with this off-comer.

Town End was originally built as a small inn called the Dove and Olive Branch in the seventeenth century, hence its later name Dove Cottage. It is a two up four down in thick stone, with small windows and oak panelling, all of which combine to make it rather dark on the ground floor. At the time, one gable end was dressed in ivy while the front of the cottage was "smothered" in roses. At the rear is a sloping terrace garden, so steep that it starts at the first floor before stretching up into Bracken Fell.

The reception by the Wordsworths was warm with, apparently, no lingering ill-feeling about the Cintra pamphlet and, as if to prove it, De Quincey was invited to lodge at Allan Bank while he waited for a housekeeper. It was certainly very handy for the Wordsworths to have De Quincey installed in their cherished former home, and their ties with the cottage may have contributed to the continuing close friendship with the new resident. Town End was used as a holiday retreat when De Quincey was away, and his sprawl of books became the Lakers' local library. Coleridge often had as many as five hundred of De Quincey's books at Allan Bank, and he invested the pages with a cornucopia of brilliant, scribbled notation —an imposition that would have delighted De Quincey. Carefree and good-humoured exploitation was the hallmark of Coleridge's attitude, but not Wordsworth's. He was a little more ambivalent.

When De Quincey arrived Dorothy remarked that "it is a great pleasure to us all to have access to such a library, and will be a solid advantage to my brother." But William had scant regard for books or bookishness, with the exception of Shakespeare, Milton and a few others. Slavish bookworming was against all his poetic principles, yet it was obviously pleasant to have the reference on hand all the same. His own library was a modest collection of a couple of hundred volumes, evidently for use not show. Most were badly bound, others not at all and a few were mutilated. In later years Southey, who had an extensive collection of foreign literature, warned De Quincey that "to introduce Wordsworth into one's library, is like letting a bear into a tulip-garden." Nature, not the printed word, was Wordsworth's avowed tutor. "Thousands of books, that have given rapturous delight to millions of ingenuous minds," said De Quincey, "for Wordsworth were absolutely a dead letter."[1]

For a man who despised extravagance, Wordsworth could be thoughtless when it came to the possessions of others; although at the time his contempt amused De Quincey. Once, while eating buttered toast at Town End, Wordsworth picked up an unread copy of Edmund Burke and permanently stained the paper by cutting the pages with his greasy knife. It was a cheap book, so the act gave De Quincey a rich anecdote instead of a grudge — but the book could have been an irreplaceable rarity. Perhaps the poet was trying to teach his disciple a lesson for his scholarly, magpie habits? If so, it did not work. De Quincey looked upon the offence with benign tolerance; after all, Wordsworth's genius excused his impatience so who could expect him to wipe his knife? The only reservation De Quincey noted was his apparent narrowness, a strange fault for a literary god.

"Very few books sufficed him," wrote De Quincey; "he was careless habitually of all the current literature, or indeed of any literature that could not be considered as enshrining the very ideal . . . In this extreme limitation of his literary sensibilities, he was as much assisted by that accident of his own intellectual condition — viz., extreme, intense, unparalleled onesidedness (einseitigkeit) — as by any peculiar sanity of feeling."[2]

Once again, this was not so much a minor source of friction as a hint of the two entirely different personalities of De Quincey and Wordsworth: it was a disagreement on first principles. In a way, neither had ever really come clean with each other. Dorothy had, in the first steps of friendship, exulted over "the power of my brother's poems over a lonely and contemplative mind, unwarped by any established laws of taste . . . a pure and innocent mind."[3] It was the idea in which everyone wanted to believe, but it was patently untrue. Dorothy's comment endorsed Wordsworth's poems as practical instruments of education and cast De Quincey as untainted innocence. No doubt De Quincey wanted Wordsworth to see him in that light, but the disciple was well-read, held sophisticated literary opinions and had more worldly experience than he cared to mention. He entered the Wordsworth fold, not under false pretences, but by glossing the truth; his admiration for the poet was unwavering and he simply did not want anything to spoil it. Wordsworth basked in De Quincey's initial admiration and relished the thought of his poems instructing and guiding the young; it was proof of his purpose and there could be no compromise. "If this opinion be erroneous," wrote Wordsworth, "I can have little right to the name of a Poet."[4] In this light, he can hardly be blamed for reacting so keenly to De Quincey's first approaches and waiving early restraint.

Life in Grasmere settled, with few ripples, to a smooth contentment. De Quincey gaily saw in New Year 1810 with a firework party at Town End to which all the local children were invited. In quieter moments he planned projects or read voraciously with a decanter of laudanum at hand. De Quincey amused himself with "the great classical circumnavigations of the earth" and all the prose works of Milton. He browsed through economic systems, which planted a seed of challenge that was soon buried by further reading and speculation. How about becoming a great philosopher and nudging Kant off his pedestal? De Quincey thought about bravely launching into an ambitious work called Emendatione Humani Intellectus (On the Correction of the Human Intellect), which naturally progressed no further than a dream of critical glory. It was a time of ferment while De Quincey tried to crack the next of his constituents of happiness —the great intellectual project. Free from opium addiction and money worries, his immediate future seemed bright.

One of De Quincey's Lake friends was also a disciple of Wordsworth, though a less obvious satellite than himself. John Wilson lived nine miles away at Elleray, Windermere, and at the age of eighteen had written to Wordsworth praising the Lyrical Ballads. Apart from the shared adoration of the poet and a love of walking, De Quincey and Wilson seemed to have little in common. One was small, wordy and sensitive while the other was exuberant, rich and wild. A true marriage of opposites.

Wilson, the son of a Scottish cloth manufacturer, was full of physical and mental energy. Although he went to Magdalen College, Oxford, at the same time De Quincey was at Worcester, it was natural that they should not have met as students. Wilson won poetry prizes and picked fights with local boxers while De Quincey wrestled with the intricacies of Kant. On leaving Oxford, Wilson bought the Elleray estate and pursued the country life. It was no idle boast when he called himself the "Admiral of the Lakes"; he commanded his own fleet of seven yachts, a ten-oared barge and several smaller craft on Windermere. Once, Wilson persuaded Wordsworth to join a fishing party that turned out to be a posse of ten ponies and thirty two people, including ten servants, who camped for a week at Wastwater. His was a life of anecdote and wish fulfilment. De Quincey's favourite tale was how Wilson had beaten up a Frenchman after an argument in a theatre, which just shows how far magnetism can excuse loutish behaviour: De Quincey usually abhorred violence. The odd couple may even have watched a main of cocks together, and one celebrated fight is known to have taken place in Wilson's drawing room on specially laid turf.

If De Quincey was in search of another hero, he had certainly found one, struck in a strangely similar mould to his brother William. But instead of the welter of contempt lavished by his brother, De Quincey now found respect. Wilson liked De Quincey for the very qualities he lacked himself, and in return he gave his little friend the full joy of living life in immediacy. In a later portrait De Quincey romantically compared Wilson to Robin Hood because he found him a chivalrous character who never declined a challenge, and yet was frequently beaten. In short, Wilson was a thoroughly likeable rogue. At Allan Bank he was known as "The Beau" because of his love of dancing, and he always told Wordsworth that he owed to him the preservation of "the best part of his nature." This nature was difficult to keep in check. De Quincey noted that "it was somewhat unusual to find that so rare an assemblage of endowments had communicated no tinge of arrogance to his manner, or at all disturbed the general intemperance of his mind."[5]

It was a fine balance. As Editor of Blackwood's Edinburgh Magazine, Wilson did De Quincey a favour by encouraging his writing and providing both a source of money and a literary outlet after his Editorship of The Westmorland Gazette. Blackwood's Magazine was founded, like the Gazette, in opposition to a Whig publication, but there the likeness ended.

It was a brilliant scandal sheet which thrived on Wilson's sharp, fearless aggression and his team of talented writers. The first number carried a swashbuckling attack on Coleridge and a society satire that whipped up a confetti of law suits and, of course, a dedicated readership. A typical example of Wilson's careless expansiveness was his election to the Chair of Moral Philosophy at Edinburgh University when, three months before he was supposed to take up lecturing duties, he wrote to De Quincey in desperation. He knew nothing about the subject, had only competed to spite a political rival and would rather like a reading list. The two friends fell out the following year, partly because De Quincey persistently missed deadlines, and partly because Wilson's brave sensationalism turned to an alleged unprincipled malice. De Quincey claimed Wilson wrote abusive reviews in one issue and expected him to counter them in the next.

However, in the Lakes, Wilson was a boon companion. Despite the fact that he had recently married, there was no shackle on his roaming style of life. Wilson went off walking with De Quincey and in 1809 they hiked to Penrith via Kentmere and Haweswater. It was Wilson who had vaguely proposed a walking tour in Spain shortly before De Quincey's arrival at Town End, and although the plan was abandoned, it was the closest De Quincey ever got to venturing abroad. When Wilson hit money problems in 1813, De Quincey lent him £200. But the gift could do nothing to deflect the ultimate disaster when, two years later, Wilson discovered that an uncle had mismanaged his £20,000 fortune. As a result, he was forced to leave Windermere and read for the bar in Edinburgh. This move from the Wordsworth circle was eventually to prove an invaluable lifeline to the personal and literary development of his friend, De Quincey.

In total contrast to the confidence of Wilson was the nervous sensibility of Charles Lloyd, a Quaker who entertained literary and artistic figures at his home, Low Brathay, at Windermere. He was prone to a violent paranoia and ended up in a Birmingham asylum where he was grossly mistreated. During periods of sanity, Lloyd was something of minor poet who attached himself to higher intellectual endeavours by holding soirées for Wordsworth, Charles Lamb, Coleridge and other notables. He hosted John Constable on his only trip to the Lakes, before the artist fled home in a state of shock at the violent storms he saw crashing across the fells. But most guests could not resist paying Lloyd a second visit, quite simply because he had the best dances and parties in town.

Despite his generosity, the humble host did not find ready acceptance by Wordsworth or Coleridge. They despised him for his effeminacy and Coleridge held a private grudge for Lloyd's novel Edmund Oliver, which drew unfavourably on Coleridge's own life story. De Quincey was more accommodating. At ten o'clock in the evening De Quincey often walked the five miles to Lloyd's home where they would sit in conversation until the early hours of the morning. They shared a sharp critical intelligence and an excessive desire for approval from those they imagined to be their intellectual superiors. For the two outsiders, the Wordsworth circle was an obvious topic of discussion.

De Quincey believed that Lloyd's strict Quaker upbringing had left him with a "legacy of woe" and had repressed natural feeling — even at his own dances Lloyd took his pleasure from watching others rather than participating. This conditioned depression was a rich vein in his poetry which De Quincey wistfully dubbed "true solitary sighs wrung from his meditative heart by excess of suffering."[6] Here, De Quincey could find a deep affinity, for he truly thought that such intensity was the only way to fully experience life. He had pushed himself to misery in London and now he watched Lloyd driven helplessly into a fate many times worse.

"Either the human being must suffer and struggle, as the price of a more searching vision," wrote De Quincey, "or his gaze must be shallow and without intellectual revelation."[7]

Both Lloyd and De Quincey were highly sensitive, even touchy, and it was this characteristic that set them apart from the masculine, Northern brusqueness of Wordsworth. As a Quaker in the traditional, drab garb, Lloyd suffered the ridicule of strangers when he ventured outside Westmorland, though sadly he was mentally ill-equipped to deal with scorn. De Quincey pinpointed with such meticulous accuracy the sort of gauntlet that Lloyd was sometimes forced to run that he perhaps revealed his own secret fear of mockery.

"Laughing outright is bad, but still *that* maybe construed into a determinate insult that studiously avows more contempt than is really felt; but tittering is hell itself; for it seems mere nature, and absolute truth, that exhorts this expression of contempt in spite of every effort to suppress it."[8]

Ether and opium diluted Lloyd's irritability, but he was constantly aware of his advancing insanity and found it impossible to cheat himself into happiness or comfort. The sound of his children innocently laughing could reduce him to tears, and pathetically, Lloyd asked to be watched for his own good.

De Quincey was once disgusted with Wordsworth for cutting him out of a conversation with Southey about the severity of Lloyd's illness by saying that details were only to be communicated to "near friends of the family."

"This to me! — O ye gods! — to me, who knew by many a hundred conversations how disagreeable Wordsworth was both to Charles Lloyd and to his wife," fumed De Quincey.[9] Wordsworth obviously thought himself "near" because his brother Christopher had married Lloyd's sister Priscilla; but even so the snub was unwarranted. However, when Lloyd escaped from the Birmingham asylum he ran to his true friend, De Quincey, assured of confidence and sympathy. During this final, brief meeting Lloyd told of the horrors of the asylum, where a keeper beat him to the ground every time he voiced any speculative subject. Incredibly, the asylum governors thought his lively intellect was directly connected with mental disease, and so they decided to thrash him back to health. When Lloyd was finally free he took his wife and children to France, but unfortunately he suffered a relapse and was incarcerated again.

The Wordsworths' ties to Town End were stronger than De Quincey had ever imagined. When he set about pruning the rambling bushes which erupted around the perimeter of his orchard, he prompted a massive reaction. Dorothy Wordsworth and Sara Hutchinson were horrified at this destruction of a cultivated, wildlife refuge, but moreover by the wilful act of someone whom they considered no more than a caretaker of the beloved home. As far as De Quincey was concerned, he only wanted a better crop of apples; but if he thought this was a petty domestic quarrel that would soon blow over, he was very much mistaken. Dorothy refused to speak to him and Sara affected a sneering contempt. Six years later, when De Quincey took his bride to Town End, Dorothy managed to write pettishly, "they . . . are now spending their honeymoon in our cottage."[10]

Luckily, at the time of the quarrel, De Quincey had no need to rely solely on the society of the Wordsworths. Just as he had probed the ways and means of ordinary folk in London markets, he now mingled freely with the dalesmen of the Lakes, driven by his insatiable curiosity. His favourite event was the auction sale, a major social rendezvous for those who farmed in remote areas. There, De Quincey could watch the "humours" of the scene as a respected and welcomed guest, while women swapped news over tea and men quaffed mugs of pow-sowdy — a blend of ale, spices and spirits that was usually brewed specially for the occasion. He loved them all and delighted in their lives.

"There you saw all ages and both sexes assembled; there you saw old men whose heads would have been studies for Guido; there you saw the most colossal and stately figures amongst the young men that England has to show; there the most beautiful young women."[11]

The simple proof of his love for these shy, polite and dignified people is that he broke all convention and eventually married one. He became deeply involved in local life, and while Wordsworth found inspiration in the drama of the landscape, De Quincey found his in the warm, human drama of the village. He professed critical views on the shape of valleys, preferring the flat-bedded Lakeland ones to the steeper-sided versions in Wales, but these ideas were Wordsworth's cast-offs. What really spurred De Quincey to originality was his observation of people, and it did not take him long to make a major phililogical discovery by listening to his neighbours' dialect.

After a long, hot August walk he took shelter from the sun in a farmhouse and chatted to a Westmorland statesman farmer about typical "pastoral" subjects such as Napoleon and the National Debt. In a corner of the cool stone building was a teenage girl nursing a baby, both oblivious to the political discussion. "I was struck by the words, *'No more Patten'* repeated two or three times and accompanied with a playful gesture as though defending her bosom from the busy little hands of the laughing infant,"[12] remembered De Quincey. When he queried the word 'Patten,' the old statesman merely chuckled and the girl blushed. But after pressing his case, and a little research, De Quincey discovered that 'to wean a child from the breasts,' translated into the Danish 'at vaenner et barn fra Patten'. The breakthrough was like the first crack in a dam—Danish words tumbled at him from all sides. When a servant girl asked her master, "Is I to sweep *attercops* off them books?" the reference to Danish spiders *('eddercops')* was obvious to De Quincey who had picked up a smattering of the language from Pink. He was thrilled with his theory that Westmorland dialect was laced with fragments from the language of Viking settlers. He offered Wordsworth an account of the origin of the language of the Lake District for an appendix in the early version of the poet's Guide to the Lakes, but Wordsworth turned him down. According to De Quincey, Wordsworth, "who never liked to be obliged to anybody for anything, declined it in his usual haughty and discourteous manner."[13] This was the second time the poet had rejected a literary contribution from De Quincey; the first snub was during the Cintra marathon when De Quincey wrote a special note on the siege of Saragossa. Yet all was not lost. The theories greeted the public through the pages of The Westmorland Gazette in a series of four articles in 1819, shortly after De Quincey's Editorship.

Only three years after settling in his rural idyll, De Quincey could see an ominous threat to his dream: he was running out of money. In the Spring of 1812 he set off for London and, like most young men of his time with cash problems, decided to follow law. He entered the Middle Temple in June but did not study very hard and only just managed to keep terms. Coleridge, smarting after a humiliating breach with Wordsworth, was also in town and still quite a star in the society firmament.

De Quincey saw Coleridge daily and joined him on the round of parties. On one memorable evening they met, as De Quincey enthused, "Lord Nelson's Lady Hamilton — the beautiful, the accomplished, the enchantress!"[14] She performed a scene from Macbeth to general acclaim and won every heart in the room. Another diversion that suitably inflamed passions was a cheering blaze. De Quincey recalled drinking tea with Coleridge and friends in Berners Street when the cry of 'Fire!' brought them sharply down from the heady plane of tea, toast and Plotinus. They "rushed out, eager for the spectacle"[15] of an Oxford Street piano-maker's store engulfed in flames. Both men enjoyed the sensuous pleasure of a good fire, even if the tinder was someone else's livelihood. It was a popular sport for the literary lion and his cub to stand back and deliver critical opinions on the respective merits of any blaze. De Quincey was well aware of the moral difficulty this posed, and he defended Coleridge. "Virtue was in no request. On the arrival of the fire engines, morality had devolved wholly on the insurance office. This being the case, he had a right to gratify his taste. He had left his tea. Was he to have nothing in return?"[16] In this particular case, he received very little. The piano-maker would surely have been disappointed to learn that his store did not live up to expectations of a "conflagration of merit". A few days after the spectacle Coleridge and friends delivered their esteemed opinions, and the fire was unanimously damned.

Shortly before De Quincey was to enter the Middle Temple he received a letter from Dorothy. It was the first step towards healing the fractured friendship, but at a dreadful cost — Catherine Wordsworth was dead.

Catherine was De Quincey's favourite of the Wordsworth

children for many complicated reasons. She was the ugly duckling of the family who had, wrote Dorothy, "not the least atom of beauty except a healthy complexion." Her plainness inspired De Quincey with love and pity in the same way that the repulsiveness of the Hall twins had attracted him as a boy. Kate called him 'Kinsey', the best pronunciation of his name she could muster, and when De Quincey was away she would search the whole house for him. The relationship reinforced De Quincey's ties to his childhood and evoked sweet memories of the cluster of sisterly affection of his earliest years.

In the spring of 1810 Kate ate some raw carrots that caused severe convulsions and left her partly paralysed down her right hand and leg. She had a limp for the rest of her brief life. Two years after the first illness, when the Wordworths had hopes of her making a recovery, she was seized with another fit of convulsions and died.

Just as Elizabeth and Jane had been snatched away, so too was Kate. De Quincey was shaken to his very core by this experience of history repeating itself.

". . . the deep, deep tragedies of infancy, as when the child's hands were unlinked for ever from his mother's neck, or his lips for ever from his sister's kisses, these remain lurking below all, and these lurk to the last."[17]

The extremity of De Quincey's emotion was revealing, even taking into consideration the similarity of the loss of his beloved Elizabeth. His recollections in letters to Dorothy were confessions of an intense kinship with an undeniable sexual element. He transformed himself from an avuncular figure into a star-crossed lover.

"Many a time, when we were alone, she would put her sweet arms about my neck and kiss me with a transport that was even then quite affecting to me. Nobody can judge from her manner to me before others what love she shewed to me when we were playing or talking alone. On the night when she slept with me in the winter, we lay awake all the middle of the night — and talked oh, how tenderly together: when we fell asleep, she was lying in my arms; once or twice I awoke from the presence of her dear body: but I could not find in my heart to disturb her.

Many times on that night — when she was murmuring out tender sounds of endearment, she would lock her little arms with such passionateness round my neck — as if she had known it was to be the last night we were ever to pass together."[18]

Such behaviour, apparently followed in all innocence, was an opportunity to love and be loved without threat or hurt, and also a chance to relive childhood with a sister substitute. It was all perfectly harmless — until Kate died. Then De Quincey began to jump to conclusions. He wrongly believed that not only was Kate's death a carbon copy of his own family tragedies, but that the circumstances were the same, too. In response, he privately accused servant Sarah Green of neglect, because she had been minding the children when Kate ate the carrot, and he claimed that his housekeeper Mary Dawson had spoken harshly to the child. In this way, the loss of Kate dug out the long buried horrors of a servant's brutality to his dead sister Jane and his rebuffed attempts to grieve for Elizabeth.

The solitary respects De Quincey had paid in the shimmering bedroom where Elizabeth had lain before burial were obviously a haunting memory as he mourned in London, divorced from Kate's corpse. He believed few had the right to see her in death and was jealous of their proximity. "I fear that the custom of the country would oblige you to let many idle gazers look at our darling's face after she was dead," he wrote to Dorothy, "but you would not I am sure, permit this if it could be avoided . . ."[19]

When he returned to Grasmere, De Quincey, for once, was allowed to grieve without any interference from family or friends. This freedom led to excessive exhibitions. For months he stole out to the village churchyard at night and stretched himself out on top of Kate's grave. But De Quincey's indulgence in such displays and fantasies resulted in him idealising Kate's memory beyond all recognition. It was the typical fate of all the womenfolk who had ever moved him: Elizabeth, Ann of Oxford Street, and now Kate. He relished the ecstasy of his experience and did all he could to heighten the luxury. Although it was a deliberate device, it was not an indication of insincerity; rather it was a purging of all De Quincey had not been able to shed on the deaths of his sisters.

At this time De Quincey experienced hallucinations and fancied he saw Kate walking across fields carrying a basket on her head and dressed in the blue bed-gown and black skirt of Westmorland. On closer inspection, the little figure always resolved into tall ferns or purple foxgloves. These "noonday visions"[20] were probably eidetic visions, totally unrelated to De Quincey's opium taking which admittedly started in earnest after Kate's death. A true eidetic image is one that revives an earlier optical experience when the eye is closed, and occasionally when open. It is a faculty common to children who find difficulty discriminating between hallucinations and the general flow of normal mental images. De Quincey was certainly aware of the power of this truly photographic memory that could present him with snapshots from the Wordsworths' family album. It became another medium for his grief.

This very thorough mental convalescence ended almost as sharply as it had begun. Once the memory of Kate was resolved into a symbol of child purity, grief vanished with suspect speed. Eight months after her death, De Quincey could look upon her grave "almost with indifference,"[21] and even relics such as Kate's tiny, red Morocco shoes left him unmoved.

"The traces of her innocent features," he wrote, "were utterly washed away from my heart: she might have been dead for a thousand years, so entirely abolished was the last lingering image of her face or figure."

It is difficult to explain away the brutal honesty of the words. De Quincey had imposed the burden of his sisters' memory on Kate and lived his fantasies through her. The frenzied emotion he generated was also further evidence of his feminine sensibility, which, as Henry Crabb Robinson noted, could be mistaken for a "puling and womanly weakness." Worse still, the thrill of being accepted back into the Wordsworth fold could have given extra fire to the pleas and outbursts, which evaporated once he was again securely in favour. Whether or not the emotion was partly contrived is uncertain. Suffice to say, that De Quincey was initially mortified at Kate's death and even surprised himself when he stopped grieving so abruptly.

With Kate tucked away in body and spirit, De Quincey found a new preoccupation in his declining health. The camping outings in Grasmere graveyard had taken their toll, and De Quincey was left with a nervous disability that caused sickness, a weakness in his legs and breathing difficulties. This, he believed, was the "vengeance" of Nature for his regardless passion; so in the hot sea baths of Ilfracombe, he washed away his ailments and the last vestiges of his bitter-sweet memories of Kate. When six-year-old Thomas Wordsworth died of pneumonia six months after Kate, William wrote thoughtfully to De Quincey: "Most tenderly and truly, with heavy sorrow for you, my dear friend." It was unnecessary. De Quincey spent little time on shows of emotion for the boy after having exhausted his reserves on Kate.

Although De Quincey was now accepted again by the Wordsworths, he had lost forever their deeper affection. He had started dosing heavily with laudanum and in 1813 was on the border of addiction. In February of that year Dorothy wrote to tell Mary Wordsworth that her son John was being dragged into one of De Quincey's fantasies.

"He now goes to Mr. De Quincey for a *nominal* hour every day to learn Latin upon a plan of Mr. De Quincey's own 'by which a Boy of the most moderate attitudes may be a good latin scholar in six weeks . . .' This said nominal hour now generally is included in the space of twenty minutes; either the scholar learns with such uncommon rapidity that more time is unnecessary, or the Master tires. Which of these conjectures is the more probably I leave you to guess."[22]

De Quincey was quickly losing his usefulness. His reliability as an ever-willing literary and family assistant was fading; and after the Wordsworth's experience with Coleridge, little patience was wasted on him. The essential quality of genuine liking had never existed, and so the flimsy structure of his "friendship" with the Wordsworths was easily blown away — even by the obvious and malicious gossip of a servant.

Dorothy reported that Mary Dawson was tired of De Quincey's "meanness and greediness," an accusation that was patently untrue. In fact, Dawson had probably refused to let the Wordsworths use Town End when De Quincey was away so that she could follow her own "gadding propensity."[23] She evidently did, and was dismissed with an illegitimate child later that year. As for De Quincey's alleged meanness, the small private fortune was dwindling and forced economies.

William was also beginning to find De Quincey an irritation. He could see him following the same degenerate path as Coleridge and wanted no dealings with another junkie who never lived up to his word. De Quincey's wheedling desire to talk on equal terms with the poet was probably another piece of gravel in the gears. After five years as a disciple, De Quincey felt he was owed something more than alms bequeathed from high table. He wanted fair exchange.

Like De Quincey's impatient mother, who never gave her rambling son a chance to express himself, Wordsworth was intolerant of his disciple's critical opinions and often blatantly ignored him. Again and again, De Quincey was to be found on the lonely perimeter.

"To everybody standing outside this sacred and privileged pale Wordsworth behaved with absolute insult in cases of this nature: he did not even appear to listen; but, as if what they said on such a theme must be childish prattle, turned away with an air of perfect indifference; began talking, perhaps, with another person on another subject."[24]

What really infuriated De Quincey was the poet's dismissal of any need for justification. When challenged, William would always waive any "fending and proving,"[25] much to the chagrin of De Quincey who was always eager for an intellectual tussle. This attitude was interpreted by De Quincey as the essence of arrogance.

"Never describe Wordsworth as equal in pride to Lucifer: no; but, if you have occasion to write a life of Lucifer," he wrote, "set down that by possibility in respect to pride, he might be some type of Wordsworth."[26]

De Quincey later confessed that, after the first year of his introduction to the poet, he had not held out much hope of drawing tight the bonds of friendship. This may have been just a salve to his pride, because for five, long and fruitless years De Quincey strived so very hard for complete acceptance. Yet had he succeeded, it would have been an unnatural union. Wordsworth lived a life of spirit with a currency of black and white certainties while De Quincey was a man of the mind who was drawn to distinctions and the shifting grey sands of the tangible world. Even when De Quincey attempted brief excursions into Wordsworth's realm of landscape and nature, he was given short shrift. After relating a story about the unusual transformation of a scene above Scar Crag on a summer afternoon, De Quincey was cut by Wordsworth saying that he had seen the same misty vision many times.

In a way, the temperamental differences were mirrored by De Quincey's and Wordsworth's respective sight defects. De Quincey was acutely short-sighted and was too poorly equipped to become a landscape aficionado; the disability may also explain his tendency towards eidetic vision and hallucination. Wordsworth suffered from a disease of the eyelids rather like trachoma, spread by soldiers returning from foreign wars. The attacks prevented him from reading and writing and forced him into the solace of darkness. Wordsworth often wore green eye-shades to ease the pain, and he treated the complaint with a copper sulphate mixture; but despite these efforts, he feared imminent blindness, especially during 1810. In each case, the afflictions bolstered established predilections: De Quincey favoured books and conversation in place of landscape, and Wordsworth avoided reading.

Just as De Quincey was finally coming to terms with the limitations of his relationship with Wordsworth, and had every reason to leave Westmorland, he fell in love. The new attraction "stepped in to enchain me precisely as my previous chains were unlinking themselves and leaving me in freedom."[27]

Three miles away from Town End, at the Nab, lived seventeen-year-old Peggy Simpson, the daughter of a statesman farmer and the eldest of six children. Although her father, John Simpson, could claim venerable Westmorland ancestry back to the 14th century, Peggy was unequivocably De Quincey's social inferior. The love affair flourished, regardless of convention. De Quincey arranged midnight trysts and often rambled home from the Nab in the early hours of the morning. Once, when John Wilson called at half past one on a Sunday morning at Town End, he found no-one home. He fell asleep on De Quincey's bed and only woke on his friend's arrival at three.

Peggy was at once a child and a woman. She was ten years younger than De Quincey and had so little education that when she read The Vicar of Wakefield, she burst into tears on the horrendous discovery that the people in it were not real. Nevertheless, the mixture of motherly affection and childlike innocence embodied in Peggy was at the heart of all De Quincey's idealised figures. He had found what he had previously had to manufacture. The fact that she could not meet him on some rarefied intellectual plane was the least of his worries. "I could not, perhaps, have loved, with a perfect love, any woman whom I had felt to be my own equal intellectually, but I never thought of her in that light," he explained.[28]

Once the affair was common knowledge, Wordsworth did all he could to rescue De Quincey, and himself, from embarrassment. He sent him down to London on the pretext of overseeing the printing of a new edition of his poems in 1815; but when such tactful diversions failed, he directly intervened. William stopped the trysts by providing company on De Quincey's midnight excursions and may even have tipped off Mrs. De Quincey, who wrote to her son following information from a "high authority." Wordsworth was in a tricky position. He was not able to condone the illicit affair of an associate now that he was a respectable freeholder who also had a daughter only a few years younger than Peggy. But Wordsworth's efforts to extricate De Quincey from his happy predicament were heavy-handed and perhaps engineered more towards the saving of his own reputation than De Quincey's.

In 1814 De Quincey temporarily moved out of the

Wordsworth orbit and into a very different intellectual atmosphere. He visited John Wilson in Edinburgh, where his friend introduced him to all the leading literary stars of the day. These included the philosopher Sir William Hamilton, the biographer of Walter Scott, J. G. Lockhard and R. P. Gillies, who, like De Quincey, was forced to seek sanctuary from creditors in Holyrood at least once in his life. With such men, De Quincey found the fair exchange he had wanted of Wordsworth.

In London, Henry Crabb Robinson had described De Quincey as "a solemn man, whose conversation does not flow readily." But in Edinburgh, De Quincey shed inhibitions and found himself lionised; he entertained at length in the small hours, drugged by opium and charged with the volubility of one who finds his audience rapt. His vast learning, photographic memory and innate sense of music in language, conjured and threaded many different elements in his conversation, from butterflies and immortality, to Milton, Homer and Aquinas. And yet he was never overbearing. He slid quietly into the exchange and wove his speech like a melody, stopping to gather suggestions and additions from his friends before finding his delicate rhythms once more. Unlike Coleridge, De Quincey avoided monologues because he insisted that he wanted an active audience, not a passive one. His gracious decision to accept the offerings of others may also have had something to do with his experience of Wordsworth's hatred for "fending and proving." De Quincey did not want to ride over anyone.

He knew his own powers and with an unerring instinct he could pull together analogies and parallelisms that connected things normally considered remote. When discussion took a boring side road, he could guide the conversation back into more interesting scenery. Using these methods, he became a supreme technician of conversation and performed nightly with headline billing among his new friends. After a long apprenticeship, De Quincey was producing for the first time. It may only have been talk, but it was a focusing of his talents.

De Quincey's relationship with Peggy was finally sealed

when the woman-child found she was pregnant. It may have been a country tradition to make marriage conditional on conception, but De Quincey dithered certainly longer than was expected, even by Peggy's standards. She gave birth to a boy, who was baptised on November 15th, 1816, and was married to De Quincey by licence at Grasmere in February the following year. The delay was the subject of much gossip and sniping, and even Wordsworth could not resist poking fun.

"A marriage is expected by some; but from the known procrastination of one of the parties, it is not looked for by others till the commencement of the millenium."[29]

Such hypocritical words. With a touch of historical irony Wordsworth's own illegitimate daughter Caroline, the product of his affair with Annette Vallon at Blois in 1792, was married the day after De Quincey to a French civil servant called Jean-Baptiste Martin Baudouin. Admittedly, Caroline was the result of a twenty-one-year-old youth's impetuous passion, and Wordsworth had every intention of marrying Annette until the war with France intervened; but the fact remains that he did not. It is a false exercise to condemn Wordsworth for what he did not feel or do, but his lack of sympathy is surprising. Perhaps he was still smarting from the "disgrace" of the marriage of his forty-six-year-old brother Richard to a servant in her twenties, two years previously?

On the whole William remained tightlipped and disapproving about the whole issue of illegitimacy and marriage, but his sister wrote vicious epistles.

"Mr. de Quincey is married; and I fear I may add he is ruined. By degrees he withdrew himself from all society except that of the Sympsons of the Nab (that pretty house between Rydal and Grasmere). At the up-rouzing of the bats and the Owls he regularly went thither—and the consequence was that Peggy Simpson, the eldest Daughter of the house presented him with a son ten weeks ago, and they were married on the day of my return to Rydal, and with their infant son are now spending their honeymoon in our cottage at Grasmere. This is in truth a melancholy story! He utter'd in raptures of the beauty, the good sense, the angelic sweetness of Miss

Sympson, who to all other judgements appeared to be a stupid, heavy girl, and was reckoned a Dunce at Grasmere School; and I predict that all those witcheries are ere this removed, and the fireside already dull. They have never been seen out of doors — except after the day was gone. As for him I am very sorry for him — he is utterly changed — in appearance, and takes largely of opium."[30]

The vein of jealousy that runs through this letter comes as a shock when compared to another note Dorothy sent to Catherine Clarkson nine years before: "Mr. De Quincey . . . you would love dearly, as I am sure I do . . . he is loving, gentle and happy." It is possible that one reason for the Wordsworths' reaction to the marriage was the expectation that De Quincey would marry Dorothy. She was closer to De Quincey than William had ever been, had helped furnish his home and was admired by both De Quincey and John Wilson. Even by one of De Quincey's own accounts, the marriage to Peggy was perhaps fated rather than decided. He told his mother: "I had long been attached to a young woman, and had visited her; for some time this was undiscovered; but when it was discovered, I felt myself as much bound in honour as I was inclined by affection to marry her."[31]

But any attempt to laugh De Quincey out of 'infatuation' was doomed to failure. In true lovers' tradition, every action to drive the pair apart provoked an equal and opposite reaction. De Quincey found genuine, lasting qualities in Peggy and wanted others to see them, too. Charles Lamb was just one of the many De Quincey tried to convert. "O how funny he did talk to me about her, in terms of such mild quiet, whispering speculative profligacy," remembered Lamb. But for the most part De Quincey's efforts were in vain: "Nothing causes a greater rankling in the heart, than to find you have laid open its finer feelings and have got laughed at for your pains — the revulsion is dreadful."[32] Above all, he held a bitter grudge against the Wordsworths for their making fun of Peggy's "angelic sweetness". It was the final wedge between him and his mentor. "I may say that I perfectly hated him for his blindness," wrote De Quincey.[33]

William was indeed blind, for Peggy was a faithful and loving wife to De Quincey for twenty years. And, contrary to Dorothy's speculations, De Quincey's fireside was far from dull — it was a scene of unexceptional, domestic bliss. Peggy, a roaring fire, books, an "eternal tea-pot" and a decanter of laudanum were all framed in the portrait De Quincey wanted painted of Town End cosiness in his Confessions. This was the period De Quincey described as his "year of brilliant water", although in reality it probably only lasted a few brief months at most. Living nightmares then came to dominate his life.

The terrifying experiences were not a product of a flaring addiction to opium, but rather of the psychological battle of withdrawal. De Quincey reduced the dose and suffered, he increased it slightly for relief. In this fluctuating pattern, he hovered over withdrawal before capitulating to opium completely around 1818 and 1819.

De Quincey's women idols — Ann of Oxford Street and his sister Elizabeth — returned in distorted forms as he steadily lost his grip on the telling handholds that structure normality. Space and time hurtled into limitless expanses or imploded down to minutae. "Thousands of years I lived and was buried in stone coffins, with mummies and sphinxes, in narrow chambers at the heart of eternal pyramids. I was kissed, with cancerous kisses, by crocodiles, and was laid, confounded with all unutterable abortions, amongst reeds and Nilotic mud."[34]

He avoided sleep and tried to cheat the visions out of his life. By asking his family to sit around him and talk, he hoped to rest in daylight hours; but the night lay forever patient, assured of its victim. The invasion of visions was so intense that De Quincey's life became inverted; his real world turned steadily inward toward the appalling confusion of night rather than the pale waiting room of day. Peggy woke De Quincey from his sleeping groans, begging to know what had frightened him, and indeed her. De Quincey came down from the dizzy, aerial architecture scratched up by a lunatic Piranesi and found himself in the quiet sobriety of his Grasmere bed, fixed solidly in time and space.

While De Quincey was chasing the enemies of his own

making in private, outside, far outside, another confrontation was calling. It was a political confrontation that would force De Quincey to think outside himself and engage in a cause. The election of 1818 was becoming an interesting proposition, with a Radical threatening the Tory county bastion. In time, The Westmorland Gazette would be established to fight the good fight; and De Quincey would be steering the flagship into battle.

Chapter Five

Government Property and High Tories

> *"For why? Because the good old rule*
> *Sufficeth them; the simple plan,*
> *That they should take, who have the power,*
> *And they should keep who can."*
> *William Wordsworth, Rob Roy's Grave.*

By 1818 Wordsworth was a much changed man. Gone was the missionary republican zeal of 1794 when he had planned a newspaper called The Philanthropist as a lantern to all men who believed monarchy was doomed and revolution at hand. "I am of that odious class of men called democrats," wrote the twenty-four-year-old Wordsworth, "and of that class I shall forever continue."[1] But the Angry Young Man made a stunning volte-face and swore his allegiance to landed gentry and the Constitution; his attitude to reform hardened and he cultivated an exaggerated fear of the Mob. When the reigning Tory landowners of Westmorland, the Lowthers, were threatened by the election challenge of the Radical Henry Brougham, Wordsworth dived into the political scrum, postponed his poetry, and fought for the good of King, Constitution and the Church. He became an undercover spy and political activist for the very cause he had formerly reviled. These new passions lost him friends and respect, but guaranteed the protection of a wealthy patron.

The cause of Wordsworth's change was the failure of the French Revolution to live up to naive expectations. The ancien regime had been toppled only to be replaced by mob tyrants and finally by the dictatorship of Napoleon. This serial disaster for liberty stoked the embers of Wordsworth's political fire into a hatred for foreign tyranny, a love of national independence and a fear of the Mob. It even prompted him to join the Ambleside Volunteers. Over a period of twenty years he became the Establishment's staunchest supporter and came to believe that quick or violent changes in society would never be possible, nor desirable.

In Britain, the shock of the Revolution threw the Tories into fearful retrenchment as they sensed that similar catastrophe was preparing to leap the Channel; there was food rioting all over Britain, and on one memorable occasion the King, himself, was hauled from his coach in St. James' Park. The reaction brought the restraints and coercion of the Two Acts of 1795/96, the Four Acts of 1817 and the Six Acts of 1819, which provided the government with the ideal machinery to quash insurrection and agitation.

The Acts made it possible to speak and write as well as perpetrate treason, and to commit a High Misdemeanour by inciting hatred of the government. All secret associations and trade unions were banned, and printing presses were censored by registration. Tavern keepers were warned to close their doors to reform societies and report names of Republicans. By 1819 the government had endeavoured to quash all attempts to incite mobs at mass meetings, or seduce the literate with pamphlets.

Tory politicians argued that this was not a limitation of freedom but, in fact, a defence of that very virtue by preservation of the State against subversion.

Any sign of revolution in England was thwarted by the strong hold of the landowners and the slow movement of ideas through a population, ten out of eleven of whom were still completely uneducated. Even so, it was only when war broke out with the French that patriotism overruled home grievances in the mind of the common man.

Other reasons for the change in Wordsworth, apart from the outcome of the Revolution in France, were a deepening pessimism caused by successive deaths in the family and an improvement in his own social status. By 1818 he was a freeholder and civil servant, favoured by the ruling county gentry. This good fortune of patronage which fell upon Wordsworth in the 1800's, may have been directly related to the mistreatment William's father had experienced at the hands of the Lowthers, and could possibly be interpreted as the guilty pay off.

Sir James Lowther, who became the Earl of Lonsdale in 1784, rightly earned his nickname 'Wicked Jimmy' by being mean and acquisitive; he managed to gather enough rotten boroughs, by buying up property and bullying freeholders, to control nine seats in Parliament. Wordsworth's lawyer father was employed by Wicked Jimmy as a political agent to push forward the frontiers of the Lowther empire by seeking loyalties and ensuring they were paid at the appropriate election. The strategy worked a treat. Cumberland and Westmorland were the Lowthers' unquestioned feudal estate as they used their riches to exploit the relentless march of the Industrial Revolution into the North of England. The prime example of the family influence was that Whitehaven became the most important port in the country after London.

When Wordsworth's father, John, died in 1783 he left five orphans and estate worth over £10,000, most of which was a pile of debts owed to him, including £4,625 by the Lowthers. A civil action dragged on for seven years while the Wordsworths tried to claim their inheritance. But even when the Wordsworths won the case at Carlisle Assizes, the Lowthers refused to pay and the dispute went to arbitration. It was only when Wicked Jimmy died in 1802 that the debts began to be paid off. Lord William Lowther, later to become the Second Earl of Lonsdale, inherited bad bills and bad feeling, but did his best to change both, and in the years to come he kept a benign eye on Wordsworth and helped him whenever possible.

In the Spring of 1806 an attractive little estate came up for sale at Ullswater. Broad How was a small farm of nineteen acres which, as Wordsworth admitted, "had little to recommend it but its own beauty." Despite the estate's lack of practical appeal William fell in love with the spot and decided to buy it. He offered £800, but the rector of Patterdale was also interested and pushed the price up to £1,000. William had no more to offer and asked the rector to withdraw from the sale. He refused.

A friend of William's, Thomas Wilkinson, who was acting on the poet's behalf in the deal, approached Lord Lowther for help. In a delicate little exchange, Lowther told Wilkinson to pay £1000 to the owner, tell Wordsworth the price was only £800 and collect the difference from himself. William learnt of the deal and was naturally upset, if only because it challenged his notions of frugality rather than compromise. Lord Lowther paid £800 into William's account but the poet refused all except the £200 necessary to secure the property. William may have saved his pride but not his position; he became a Westmorland freeholder and earned the right to vote thanks to this discreet gesture by the local aristocrat. Although William was already a Cumberland freeholder after Sir George Beaumont gave him an estate at Applethwaite, near Keswick, in 1803, this latest gift was particularly important. It soothed the Lowther family conscience for former misdeeds, bought a friendly vote and was the first of several useful investments in Wordsworth.

The Lowther debt, which finally amounted to about £3,000 shared between William and Dorothy, was paid off and invested unprofitably in property near Penrith by William's brother Richard. By 1812 William had money problems again. Exasperated that the annual income from his poems amounted to no more than seven pounds, he considered rattling off a pot-boiler. But first he wrote to Lord Lowther, now the Earl of Lonsdale, to ask for a job.

Lord Lonsdale said he could come up with nothing immediately, but offered William £100 a year until an appointment was available; Wordsworth refused the gift but accepted later in the year. He was now directly in the pay of the Lowthers and was looking forward to a secure post. In this way, he was cushioned against the stringencies of eking out a living solely on his poetic product, but also in the dangerous position of being used like his father. William found this latter fear unthinkable.

William regularly visited Lowther Castle, where he met "heaps of fine folks", including Prince Frederick of Orange, and found his transition to High Toryism more comfortable than he could ever have expected. Here was an aristocrat who used his wealth wisely, patronised the arts (Hogarth and Boswell were both encouraged by the Lowthers) and cared passionately for the security, or rather status quo, of the county. Wicked Jimmy was long dead.

In March 1813 William followed in the illustrious footsteps of Chaucer, Spenser and Milton. He became a government employee and was graced with the grand title of 'Head Distributor of Stamped Vellum Parchment and Paper within and for the County of Westmorland and Part of the County of Cumberland.' Although much has been made of the similarity of Wordsworth's position to those of the aforementioned poets, the only common denominator is that each became civil servants. Chaucer was clerk of works to Edward III, Spenser was secretary to Lord Grey and Milton was secretary to Cromwell — by comparison Wordsworth's post was chaff. As some of his friends noted, William was "marked as government property"[2] rather than distinguished by his promotion to minor officialdom.

Despite popular rumour, William's job was not a sinecure. He had to collect Inland Revenue duties on all legal documents from licences for lace-dealers, to books, paper and insurance policies. Stamps were bought from sub-distributors, often market town tradesfolk, and the head distributor usually made quarterly rounds to collect receipts and forward them to London. The pay was about £400 a year, but William employed a secretary-cum-accountant to help with the book-keeping. Taking into account the £100 pension paid to his predecessor, this left William with little over £200 a year.

The post of distributor also threw up the odd squalid crisis in the face of William. He had to sell up one of his subs at Kirkby Lonsdale who was arrested for debt while owing William £300. Frightened that the debt might be transferred to himself, William searched the sub's house, sold his belongings and found a hoard of legacy receipts in a swill basket.

By the winter of 1817 William wanted to expand his distributorship and fancied adding the North Cumberland district to his already substantial area. He negotiated with Lord Lonsdale and even agreed to pay off the present distributor with a £350 annuity. However, the transaction was called off because Wordsworth thought it would expose himself and the Lowthers to charges of political corruption. The 1818 election was looming large and Wordsworth wanted to play a full part. Lord Lonsdale was as keen as ever to oblige Wordsworth, and in 1817 he offered William the Collectorship of Customs at Whitehaven, a post his uncle, Richard Wordsworth, had held. William rejected the offer mainly because he wanted to continue living in Rydal.

As William's personal security increased, he became aware of the disintegration of the surrounding rural world. He was now suspicious of the mysteries of social change and unrest, and he placed his faith in the stabilising influence of land ownership, which, in his eyes, became England's last bastion. He confided his fears to Daniel Stuart in April 1817.

"The agricultural population of Cumberland and Westmoreland is at present sound; but I would not engage that it will continue so, in case rebellion should get the upper hand in other parts of the Island. A Revolution will, I think, be staved off for the present nor do I even apprehend that the disposition to rebellion may not without difficulty be suppressed, notwithstanding the embarrassment and heavy distresses of the times. Nevertheless, I am like you, an alarmist, and for this reason, I see clearly that the principal ties which kept the different classes of society in a vital and harmonious dependence upon each other have, within these 30 years either been greatly impaired or wholly dissolved. Everything has been put to market and sold for the highest price it would bring. Farmers used formerly to be attached to their Landlords, and labourers to their Farmers who employed them. All that kind of feeling has vanished — in like manner, the connexion between the trading and landed interests of country towns undergoes no modification whatsoever from personal feeling, whereas within my memory it was almost wholly governed by it. A country squire, or substantial yeoman, used formerly to resort to the same shops which his father had frequented before him, and nothing but a serious injury real or supposed would have appeared to him a justification for breaking up a connexion which was attended with substantial amity and interchanges of hospitality from generation to generation. All this moral cement is dissolved, habits and prejudices are broken and rooted up; nothing being substituted in their place but quickened selfinterest, with more extensive views, — and wider dependencies — but more lax proportion as they are wider. The ministry will do well if they keep things quiet for the present constitution in church and state is to last, it must rest as heretofore upon a moral basis; and they who govern the country must be something superior to mere financiers and political economists."[3]

This letter gives an explicit and accurate picture of the prevailing rural atmosphere in the early 1800's. William's diagnosis is largely correct, but like many contemporary Tories, he was unable to suggest an antidote or embrace the full inevitability of what was happening. The fracture of traditional class relationships was a creeping malady that irrevocably altered the structure of society. Yeoman farmers had paid dearly for their independence and many were driven by poverty to sell or emigate to a better dream. In their place, landlords ushered in tenant farmers who employed a cheap, drifting labour force. It was a phenomenon that Wordsworth had first indentified as early as the 1790's when he composed Incidents upon Salisbury Plain about a yeoman farmer who, through "severe mischance and cruel wrong,"[4] was evicted. By 1817 such cruel wrongs were commonplace as the dictum of 'small is inefficient' spread. The yeoman farmer was either a freeholder or possessed ancient rights which allowed him to pass his small estate from father to son, so that each might have a pride in modest ownership. This inheritance was lost as the bigger landlords bought up farms and worked them with labourers who only owed allegiance to their paltry pay packets. Those who were discarded by the system found the cities, throbbing with production, only too happy to devour them.

Communal relationships evaporated in the new order of economic demand and with them, as Wordsworth rightly identified, "moral cement" was dissolving. But the overall picture was not one of worsening, or even continuous, political agitation. The climax of the revolution panic had passed by 1806, although unrest flared again from 1815 to 1820 and from 1830 to 1832. Despite this pendulum of activity the basic problems remained: industrial progress; the legacy of the war against France and the struggle of the new power against the traditional handicrafts. In this climate, Wordsworth could only think to hold fast the reins of the old world rather than look for a creative solution through social reform. When he realised that Henry Brougham was to challenge the Lowthers in the 1818 election, he rallied with the Tories not, he claimed, out of parochial self-interest, but for the general good of the country. He felt it was his unquestioned social duty. On December 20th 1817 he pledged his allegiance to Lord Lonsdale and wrote: ". . . your Lordship has only to point out the way in which you wish me to exert myself."[5] And exert himself, he did.

For over forty years the Lowther family had retained two parliamentary seats unopposed, and in 1817 these were held by Lord Lowther and Colonel Henry Lowther, sons of the Earl of Lonsdale. The upstart rival for one of the seats was Henry Brougham, a Radical and a bewitching orator, who had the dangerous gift of stirring mob audiences wherever he held meetings. Wordsworth was terrified, although he had already met Brougham on two peaceful occasions. He called Brougham "the most prominent Demagogue in the Kingdom" and "a man of desperate Fortune, ungovernable passions and prepared for any mischief."

Brougham was a wild outsider, a talented advocate, who ran freely on the left of the Whigs. He favoured legal reform and slave emancipation and had helped found the dashing Edinburgh Review, which had ridden roughshod over Wordsworth' poems with sneering abandon. In 1830 he became Lord Chancellor and supervised the passage of the 1832 Reform Bill through the Upper House. For all his

Radical leanings, Brougham had a powerful political patron in Lord Thanet, Hereditary High Sheriff of Westmorland, and originated from a family of landed gentry who owned an estate around Penrith and also carried a disturbing streak of insanity in their genes. The general line of Brougham's attack on the Lowther stronghold was the appeal for freeholders to assert their independence by voting for the 'independent' candidate and so break the family monopoly. This was not the first time that Brougham had tried to get his foot in Westmorland. In 1806 he used anti-slavery campaigner William Wilberforce to negotiate a country seat with Lord Lonsdale's approval. The interloper was rejected, and the Lowthers tightened ranks. But in 1818 Brougham no longer asked for tacit approval — he threw himself into violent opposition. Moreover, Brougham had assumed that if he failed in Westmorland he could always retreat to sit for Lord Darlington's borough of Winchelsea. But when Lord Darlington pointed out that he was related to the Lowthers, Brougham was threatened with having his escape route removed. This, of course, added an edge to his election fight and, as a Brougham supporter, Lord Lambton, commented: "He worked like a horse. He was at once candidate, counsel, agent, canvasser and orator, and changing his character every hour, and always cheerful and active."[6]

When Wordsworth returned from a visit to London in January 1818, he arrived in Kendal to see electioneering in full flood. He stopped writing poetry and got down to the serious business of gathering political intelligence. Dorothy was just as impassioned as her brother, which left only Sara Hutchinson to mourn for William's true vocation. She felt it "pitiable that William should be thus diverted from his natural pursuits."[7]

Even as William's carriage raced back to the Lakes, he was scribbling a letter, which argued that split voting would only favour Brougham. It was signed "A Friend to Consistency", and was published in the local paper, the Kendal Chronicle, before being printed as a handbill. William knew he was fast becoming a man obsessed: "You will think, dearest Sara, that my head is turned with this election, that I can think of nothing else, and true it is, the tendency of all these proceedings is evidently so dangerous, that we are interested for more than it is even possible for *you* to conceive at a distance . . ."[8]

In the coming months William collected information on his travels round the country in his official capacity as distributor of stamps. It included detailed personal profiles of those who could be converted to become the party faithful and those who should be marked down as reformers, dissenters or, perhaps worst of all, those simple souls who would derive perverse pleasure from seeing the Lowthers slighted. William related who could be bribed, who could be trusted with a freehold and how much property people owned. By the time he had gained the Earl of Lonsdale's sanction to buy an estate and create a nest of freeholds for trusted votes at Little Langdale, William was indistinguishable from his father. He was the corrupt agent of the Lowthers' rotten system of enfranchisement. According to one contemporary source, Appleby might well have been a Cornish borough because the Lowthers even scrambled to buy up pigsties that had curiously been deemed freeholds.[9] Not content with bribery, the family tried to use the land assessment list to disenfranchise opposing voters. Despite discovery of the irregularity, the tactic worked, and Brougham lost eighty votes because of errors in land tax assessments.

It took little time for people to realise the source of the anonymous letters, which appeared in papers and handbills. As early as February, Thomas Clarkson's wife warned Dorothy Wordsworth about the "predicament" of her brother's intervention. Later, Brougham's brother James said he would have Wordsworth fined £100 for having "intermeddled." But William ignored both the warning and the threat, and agitated with even greater vigour.

The Lowthers began to canvass on February 9th in Kirkby Lonsdale and two days later entered Kendal where James Brougham was enjoying success rallying the town rabble, the 'Fell-siders,' who could add voice but not votes to the occasion. Despite the competition, Lord Lowther was brimming with confidence: "Tomorrow is Gala Day. We are to enter Kendal in triumph to be attended by four hundred people."[10]

In the event, the gala turned out to be the worst riot Kendal had ever seen. The offer of free beer by the Lowthers the previous night at least explained why the streets were full of drunks swaying to the mocking chant of "Lowther ale and Brougham forever." But the cynical humour soon degenerated into brutality. Inflammatory handbills distributed by Brougham supporters aggravated fraying tempers and by the time the Lowthers were approaching Kendal, a riot was in full swing. The 'yellow' reception committee rode out of town, two abreast, to warn the procession of 131 horsemen, eleven carriages and innumerable yeomanry. But short of calling off the canvass and declaring the day for Brougham, there was little anyone could do.

The mob defended the town at Nether Bridge and the Cock and Dolphin Inn, opposite, by tearing up and smashing gritstone slabs for missiles. An opening in the rabble was made by the advance horseman charging and trampling a few stone-throwers who were too full of bravado and beer to retreat. When the procession forced through, the mob joined the Lowther yeomanry and the hail of rocks and mud continued from the rear. The cavalcade started galloping through Kirkland but then faced a line of demonstrators with placards and a complete band at Highgate. Among those bearing standards like "No Corn Bill" and "No Suspension of Habeas Corpus Act" were the journeyman printers of the Kendal Chronicle who held aloft a banner emblazoned "Brougham Forever" and, on the reverse, "Freedom of the Press." In an ill-advised fit of vainglory, the Lowther standard bearer grabbed the Brougham flags and galloped ahead. He took refuge with his trophies in the King's Arms but was forced to return them when the mob threatened to rip down the inn. Meanwhile, the main party was ambushed again, this time at Allhallows Lane.

The Lowthers finally arrived at their destination, the Commercial Inn, but some horses were so frightened that the outriders found themselves charging down Stricklandgate and out of town. Lord Lowther and Col. Lowther managed to reach the safety of the inn, although the doors were ripped off their carriage. They took their meal in the upper rooms of the inn for fear of rocks crashing through the dining room windows.

In fact, they were lucky to have any food at all because a gang of Scots and Irish navvies were camped in the kitchens eating the joints of beef that had been specially prepared for the more honoured guests. Three hundred navvies, who normally would have been working on the Kendal-Lancaster Canal, had been given the day off by the Lowthers to swell the number of family supporters. The plan had evidently gone wrong somewhere. The innkeeper got rid of the forty beef-eaters by promising them a free pint at the White Hart, just across the road. Plenty of pints and a couple of Cheshire cheeses later, the navvies were content. But outside, the Kendal mob was jealous of this good fortune and staged an assault on the inn. The navvies smashed up nineteen chairs as weapons and, although they were driven out, the first floor of the White Hart was gutted.

At the Commercial Inn, the Lowthers ate what beef was left and sent despatches to their father about the "most unfavourable reception." "We were all attacked," wrote Lord Lowther, "the carriages broke to pieces, Mr. John Fleming had two teeth knocked out and many other of our friends some hard knocks and bruises."[11]

The riots provided both sides with political capital for months, and the first screed about the chaos appeared in the Kendal Chronicle on February 21st. By now, Wordsworth, whose old schoolfriend Fleming had been hurt, was taking a keen interest in the local Press — and its apparent bias.

The first Kendal newspaper was published by the town's first printer, Thomas Cotton, in 1731 at No. 11 Finkle Street, and was called The Kendal Weekly Courant. It was a four page, medium quarto paper, which sold for 1½d. After Cotton, the Cowan Head papermaker Thomas Ashburner took over the Courant and changed the title to the Kendal Weekly Mercury, which was first published at the Fishmarket in January 1735 and sold for a penny. Sometime before 1745 or 1746, the Mercury was discontinued and Ashburner's son, James, filled the gap with a fortnightly, sixteen page periodical called The

Agreeable Miscellany, or, Something to Please Every Man's Taste. However, the Miscellany, with its notable account of the passing of 1,600 Scots and Northumberland rebels through Kendal, only survived 39 issues. In 1777 a sheet almanack, The Kendal Diary, was published by Pennington, the bookseller and printer, at Stricklandgate until about 1837. The weekly Westmorland Advertiser and Kendal Chronicle was established in June 1811 and sold for 6½d. At the time of the 1818 election fever, the Chronicle was the town's only newspaper and had a reliable Editor called William Abbot. But he was replaced and the paper became a mouthpiece for anti-Lowther views.

William wrote to Lord Lonsdale: "The Editorship of the Kendal paper has passed into other hands, those of a Mr. Harrison a dissenting Minister. He is inwardly against us, which is much to be regretted. The bias of his mind sufficiently appears, in the paper of this day, in the account he has given of Mr. James Brougham's reception. I am on very friendly terms with Mr. H. and could influence him, I believe, to a certain extent; but my situation requires a degree of caution which diminishes my power."[12]

William obviously thought he could manipulate the Rev. John Harrison on the strength of his attendance at the minister's Market Place Chapel. He sometimes went to service there when he stayed with his friend Thomas Cookson, who was a chapel trustee. After an especially offensive article had appeared in the Chronicle, which accused Lord Lowther of living off government sinecures and questioned the legitimacy of Col. Lowther's rank, William visited Harrison to sound his political views and demand fairplay. Naturally, a full report was sent to Lord Lonsdale.

"Much of the abuse, which to my knowledge has done a great mischief, found its way into the Paper, under the shape of Letters, often inserted for mere want of matter to fill the Columns. Being a dissenter the present Editor has naturally a strong bias to opposition, and complaint; but he is no approver of Mr. Brougham, deems him unfit to represent any county, and regards him as a trading Publican. He has refused Mr. B.

his vote and means to vote on neither side, unless (a reservation which is suspicious) he is provoked by the Intemperance of either Party." [13]

Wordsworth's solution to the problem of filling the pages of the Chronicle was to write as many letters as possible and urge his friends to do the same — if only to keep the opposition out. At the same time Lowther supporters printed yet more handbills and pamphlets, and published articles in Tory newspapers like the Carlisle Patriot.

The uncertainty about the Chronicle was caused by the composition of the proprietors. Three shares were owned by a staunch Brougham supporter, Jacob Wakefield, one by another member of the Wakefield family, one by a Mr. Swainson, a democrat, and three by friends of the Lowthers, including John Pearson, a former mayor of Kendal and a Lowther Committee member. Wordsworth was inclined to try and gain control of the existing paper rather than publish a rival, but he admitted that the Lowthers may have left the decision too late.

"Five shares out of eight of this paper are in the hands of our enemies; therefore it would avail nothing could we get the Editor over to our side. He would immediately be dismissed and a worse person put in his place . . . The paper might have been easily purchased a few weeks ago; now, if the Contest goes forward, they will not part with it. — It has done great harm; and ought to be under your Lordship's command, as soon as it can be got hold of. To set up another on different principles would at present be of no use, as the People would only read that which flattered their passions." [14]

However, even as plans were made for a Tory takeover of the Chronicle, a subscription for a new paper was being secretly drawn up. On February 19th Wordsworth assured Lord Lonsdale: "The Subscribers to the newspaper are animated by very honourable feelings; and they hope to destroy the old paper, by withdrawing advertisements from it."[15]

Although both Wordsworth and Lord Lonsdale would have preferred to persist in their attempt to buy a majority shareholding in the Chronicle, they found themselves caught up in the enthusiasm for a new paper. By late February, the Lowthers had £1,675 subscribed by 32 supporters* eager to buy part or full shares at £50 each.

The Brougham Committee heard of the scheme for a new paper and on February 28th the Chronicle proclaimed that "a deep laid plan to stifle the voice of Independence and Liberty in the County" was afoot. The Chronicle still regarded itself as impartial and was deeply offended by the plan for a Lowther paper "which is to be the organ of their own sentiments alone."[17] Apart from the ethics involved, the Chronicle proprietors were probably also worried about the effect it might have on their own paper's circulation. There was a rapid reshuffle. The Rev. Harrison was ousted from the Editor's chair and the Chronicle publisher, twenty-seven-year-old Richard Lough, who later professed to be a "glorious revolution of 1688 man," took his place. The Chronicle decided that it liked exposures, and so revealed details of Wordsworth's visit to Harrison.

". . . a friend of the opposite party informed the late Editor in the name of Lord Lowther, that perfect impartiality was all his Lordship requested and his friend proposed. The proposition appeared equitable, and was acceded to, by the Editor: but the faction, we do not say Lord Lowther, being not altogether content with perfect neutrality has resolved to establish another paper in Kendal."[18]

A week later the gloves were off, and Lough announced that he was "compelled to quit the line of neutrality" after having already received " a sufficient share of party abuse." Lord Lowther admitted that Wordsworth's attempt to reason with Harrison had failed and just as he was writing, "I almost despair of neutralising him — or getting any hold upon

*The original backers were: the Rev. John Hudson, Christopher Wilson, Edward Wilson, William Braithwaite, Joseph Braithwaite, Isaac Wilson, Thomas Harrison, Smith Wilson, Daniel Harrison, John Gandy, James Gandy junior, John Fleming, Thomas Fell, James Johnson, John Fell Swainson, Joseph Swainson Junior, Daniel Wilson, John Huddleston, Isaac Hadwen, Thomas Holme Maude, John Bolton, the Rev. William Barton, James Adam, James Bateman, James Gandy, John Harrison, George Forrest, K. Finsthwaite, Matthew Atkinson, the Rev. Harrison Shaw, Robert Shepherd Stephenson, John Hill.[16]

him,"[19] Lough took the chair. Any hope of pleading the party case had gone.

Now that a new paper seemed the surest way to promote the Lowther interest, Wordsworth consulted his old friend and the veteran newspaperman Daniel Stuart, who was joint proprietor of The Courier in London with T. G. Street. On March 9th Stuart replied with a pragmatic letter crammed with solid advice. He shared "alarmist" views with Wordsworth.

"You begin to feel the effects of Seditious publications even in your retired and hitherto tranquil district. This is but a slight symptom of the great disease so rapidly spreading, which, it is likely will one day break out with violence and destroy the Constitution."[20]

Unlike Wordsworth, Stuart could stand back and take an objective view of the practical difficulties facing anyone wanting to set up a paper in such a volatile political climate. He realised that commercial stability was the only route to success: scoring political points came later.

"Writers and writing may be found for the present election contest, hand bills and posting bills and c. may answer the present purpose; but the real object should be a permanent one; the occupation of the Newspaper Customers and the attraction of the advertisements. This well done will sink the present Kendal Paper in sale, resources and spirits. It should not be bought. That would only encourage others to spring up."[21]

Stuart suggested that the paper should be printed either at the Patriot offices in Carlisle or at the Lancaster Gazette. He preferred the latter because the paper could be distributed on the way from Lancaster to Kendal on Friday evening, before the Chronicle came out on the Saturday. In this way, he insisted that "you may have a new paper in a *week* at a very trifling expense." But he also added a postscript to his busy letter, admonishing the county Tories for their laxity.

"I recollect seeing the Kendal Paper about 15 months ago and thinking it one of the most furiously Jacobinical in the Kingdom. How happen it that all the good men of Westmorland so long slept over it?"[22]

Wordsworth was spurred into action by his friend's criticism, and he wrote to Stuart's partner, Street, and the Editors of the Sun and New Times in the hope of finding someone to edit the Kendal paper. But there was no-one they could recommend, and even those who were technically qualified turned out to be "all of bad principles." Meanwhile, the tone of the Chronicle deteriorated and prompted Wordsworth to remark: "This paper as now conducted reminds me almost at every sentence of those which I used to read in France during the heat of the Revolution."[23]

While efforts were redoubled to find an Editor, Wordsworth began work on a tract called Two Addresses to the Freeholders of Westmorland, which appeared in various forms in newspapers and was later printed as a pamphlet. These arguments against Brougham's unfitness to hold parliamentary office were soon answered when the subject of the political essay arrived in Kendal fêted as a hero.

Trumpeters, flag bearers and an escort of twenty-four horsemen heralded Brougham's triumphant Kendal entrance on March 23rd. He rode on the dickie box of his carriage waving to the crowds, despite snow and hail. Dressed in a dark coat, yellow waistcoat and blue scarf, he cut a very impressive figure.

The procession stopped at the Wakefield Bank, on Stricklandgate, and while the band played God Save the King, Brougham took his position at centre window. In a house opposite, Dorothy Wordsworth and family friends watched the spectacle. Although Dorothy may have felt a stab of shame at seeing her own cousin, William Crackenthorpe, flank Brougham, she was proud to discover that her brother's writings had begun to needle the opposition. Brougham dismissed William's political prose and accused him of holding a sinecure. "I do not speak of his poetry, but his laboured compositions in prose — which would be far harder work for his readers than the *duties* of his place furnish *him* with,"[24] Brougham dryly told the crowd. Once this harangue started, Crackenthorpe shrugged in a good-humoured manner at Dorothy before discreetly leaving the window. The gesture was unnecessary because Dorothy was really flattered by the attention Brougham devoted to William. However, her righteous indignation did manage to surface through the glow of pride. Perhaps inflamed by memories of De Quincey's orchard pruning antics, Dorothy exclaimed: "Oh! he looked ready to lead a gang of Robespierrists set to pull down Lowther Castle and tear up the very trees that adorn it."[25]

Brougham countered the "senseless cry of Jacobinism" and swore his allegiance to the Crown. That evening, the best joke of the celebration dinner at the King's Arms was reported in full, complete with misquotation, in the Chronicle. Of course, it came from the eloquent lips of Brougham.

". . . a Poet, who honoured this part of the country by residing in it, and who, he really believed, was a very good man, but made sad work of it, when he meddled in the common business of life, had written four lines on another occasion, which seemed applicable to the exorbitant pretensions of Lord Lonsdale's family, and to the resistance of the County.

'For why, the ancient simple rule
Sufficeth them, the good old plan —
That they should take who have the power,
And they should keep who can.' "[26]

De Quincey was fully aware of the importance of Wordsworth in this election fight and was sure to have known about the Tories' unproductive search for an Editor for their paper. His relations with Wordsworth had been poor to non-existent over the last year, but he roused himself from the stupors of opium to heal the wounded friendship. Instead of walking the few miles to Rydal Mount and presenting himself, De Quincey embarked on a series of letters, painstakingly and pathetically designed to win favour again. Whether the letters arose from a genuine sympathy for the political struggle, or whether they were part of a deliberate strategy culminating in an application for the Editorship, is uncertain. But De Quincey well knew that if anyone could get him the job, Wordsworth was the man.

The first letter on March 25th related an "insult to the house of Lowther" and told how the Grasmere curate, the Rev. Jackson, had allowed the bells of his church to be rung on Brougham's arrival. This outrage placed De Quincey in something of a dilemma because he had just written two pro-Lowther papers and was about to give them to Jackson to pass on to the party Committee for inspection. Did Wordsworth have any suggestions? The tone was formal but cautious and left plenty of room for manoeuvre.

In his next letter, De Quincey followed with a plea for Wordsworth to show the papers to the Lowther Committee — of course, after the poet had graciously made any revisions he thought necessary. After thus inveigling Wordsworth's assistance, De Quincey distanced himself and his wife from the known radical views of his father-in-law. He called John Simpson a "rank Jacobin" and admitted that the statesman farmer was beyond political redemption.

Once the papers were in Wordsworth's hands in April, De Quincey's letters withdrew to the neutral ground of quibbles over printing and, for a time, the self-justification faded.

Close Comments on a Straggling Speech was not just a "capital title" for De Quincey's pamphlet, as Crabb Robinson remarked, but also a well-argued and witty counter to Brougham's election address in Kendal. De Quincey worked through to the early hours of April 1st but still only managed to complete three-quarters of it. Even so, he posted what was done and hoped for the best.

It was the break he was looking for. Close Comments was very popular with Wordsworth and the Lowther Committee, and was printed in Kendal by Airey and Bellingham, who were soon to become printers of The Westmorland Gazette. The Chronicle reacted in character by dismissing Wordsworth's Two Addresses and De Quincey's Close Comments as "hullets" — meaning owlets, all feathers and no flesh — but De Quincey was delighted.

At last he was on safe ground. He was recognised as a gifted political writer with his point by point rebuttal of Brougham's speech and was now manning the barricades against Jacobinism alongside Wordsworth. De Quincey once remarked that in years to come archaeologists could dig him up and find a superb example of a "fossilised Tory." In 1818 he was beginning to prove just how fascinating a specimen he could be, given opportunity and encouragement.

On the day Wordsworth was writing to Lord Lonsdale, "the delay of the new Kendal Paper, is much to be regretted,"[27] De Quincey was tendering his application for the Editorship. According to the Rev. Jackson, Wordsworth had already turned the job down and now De Quincey detected a vacuum that he could fill.

"— do you know of any reasons which should make it imprudent or unbecoming in me to apply for it? If you do not, and there should be no other person whose interests in this case you are inclined to prefer, — I feel confident that you will do me the kindness to assist me in obtaining it with your recommendation. I must mention however, which possibly may be alone sufficient to defeat my application, that in about a year I should be under the necessity of resigning the place; having an intention then or soon after to remove finally to London for the prosecution of my profession as a lawyer. That part of an editor's duties which respects the mechanical and commercial management of a Paper — I should certainly not be competent to undertake; but perhaps this department could be conducted by some clever compositor or other person about the Press; and at any rate, with advice from a judicious man of business, I could learn even this part (which, in a place no larger than Kendal, cannot be very intricate); and, in respect to the Selection of articles from the London Papers and the Political Comments on them, I trust that I should be able to satisfy the wishes of the patriotic subscribers. In one point you may still feel some doubt of my competence to do so — judging from your former Knowledge of me; in punctuality. I mean, and power of steady perseverance: but in this I am altered since I last had the happiness to associate with you; and, among other grounds of remorse, I have suffered too much in conscience on account of time left unimproved or misemployed — ever to offend in that way again, even upon calls of less importance than this would be."[28]

It is worth noting that De Quincey would only consider the Editorship on a temporary basis because he was still under the illusion that he would finish his law studies. He offered little technical expertise but said he already had a store of articles, from translations of minor works of Kant to amusing anecdotes for the dalesman. De Quincey knew, however, that the biggest stumbling block was his reputation for bad time-keeping and so he ingratiated himself as best he could. Like the drug addict he was, he grovelled and protested that he would never offend again. The keenness of De Quincey to get this job probably owed more to the lure of a regular wage than perhaps to politics. His confession that a "trifling emolument would at this time be very useful to me" was an understatement; he already had two children and his wife was expecting a third.

This confusion of self-effacement and promotion failed to convince Wordsworth. He had faithfully considered Daniel Stuart's letter about the selection of an Editor, and had reservations about De Quincey who, as a gifted intellectual prone to histrionics, was probably not the best candidate to launch a new publication. In the light of Stuart's comments it is easy to see why De Quincey's application was rejected.

"A fit man may be found, and I should not think the worse of him were he not a Genius of a writer, if he had good sense, steadiness and integrity, he having been bred a Printer, and having a common education."[29]

Despite the sense in Wordsworth's decision, the poet played safe and, in fact, made a mistake. De Quincey was a firework of ideas for the paper and, above all, hungry for work. He even suggested setting up an appeal fund for a widow and seven children whose breadwinner had been killed in an accident at Patterdale Quarry. His scheme was born more out of exploitation than charity, for he openly admitted that he only wanted to stop Brougham and the Chronicle from getting on the bandwagon. But as far as the new paper was concerned, De Quincey's heart was in the right place.

Although The Westmorland Gazette was launched on May 23rd by a Mr. C. J. Fisher, imported from London, De Quincey contributed to the paper and showed sustained interest. It stood him in good stead, for within a few weeks Fisher was sacked and De Quincey was called in to harden the partisan line.

De Quincey experienced both domestic bliss and the hideous terror of opium nightmares at Town End. It was here that he selected news for the Gazette and wrote his articles.

Kate Wordsworth's grave at St. Oswald's churchyard, Grasmere. At night, De Quincey mourned for the child by lying on top of her grave, and weeping.

De Quincey's opium scales on which he used to weigh his drug doses.

Lost at Kendal,

DURING THE SNOW PROCESSION OF

Mr. BROUGHAM,

On MONDAY last, into Kendal,

THE CALCULATION OF THE AMOUNT OF THE

Sinecure in the Exchequer,

Which the FATHER of

H. BROUGHAM, Esq.

Of Brougham Hall.

POSSESSED FOR FORTY-FIVE YEARS,

And which enabled Him to send his Son to the University, and to give Him a Qualification for

A SEAT IN PARLIAMENT.

ALSO,

A Copy of the Appointment of Mr. WYBERG, *to the Sinecure Office of Clerk of the Peace for the*

WEST RIDING OF YORKSHIRE.

Which he Executes by DEPUTY, and for which he has RECEIVED about

40 THOUSAND POUNDS.

A Small Deal Box, containing several UNSATISFIED DEMANDS

LETTERS from G. Manners, esq.

A. Mc. KERRYL, Esq. &c.

Whoever will bring these Articles to the *Sign* of the *Bunch of White Feathers*, in Kendal, shall be rewarded in the most liberal manner.

Libellous anti-Brougham poster distributed by Lowther supporters during the 1818 Westmorland election.

MY FOURTH ADDRESS

TO THE

FREEHOLDERS

OF

WESTMORLAND!

March 18, 1818.

**From the House of the Commons, which we call *the Room*,
I address you, my slaves, I, the Orator *Brougham*.**

I have at length the pleasure, Gents.
Of telling you of my intents—
To-morrow, I set out from Town,
And upon Monday shall be down.
How great will be *your* Happiness
To see *me*, easily I guess.
But hear now what I have to say,
Nor *fail* my *Mandate to obey*—

As I've but fourteen days to spare,
To wait on *you*, too much it were—
Your Roads are bad, your Hills are high,
Climb them who chooses, 'tw'ont be I-!
But tho' it is beneath *my* state
On all or each of *you to wait*—
There's no good reason that I see,
To *check* your waiting upon *me*—

And hence I this, my notice send,
To which you're order'd to attend—
On such a Day, at such an Hour—
I'm to be seen from twelve to four,
But 'ere your Cities I shall reach,
Thousands must follow at my Breech,
Whilst some my entrance, more to deck,
Must put the Halter round their neck,
And do the work of Horse, or Ass,
For thus thro' all your Streets I'll pass—

I thus have notified my Orders,
On Monday I shall cross your Borders;
And having said what's most expedient,
I am, meantime, your most obedient

Henry Brougham.

Lowther election poster masquerading as one distributed by Brougham. It pokes fun at the way Brougham's carriage was hauled by supporters into each town on his canvass.

An early Stanhope Press used in De Quincey's day by the Gazette printers Airey and Bellingham. The model was popular with printers, even though the wooden frame of the press tended to split under pressure.

KENDAL, 7th JULY, 1818.

An Advertisement, dated **Lowther Committee-Room,** Appleby, 4th July, **1818**, having been published, whereby **Mr. C. J. Fisher**, who calls himself the **Editor** of the *Westmorland Gazette*, announces that an *Extraordinary* or *Supplementary Gazette* is intended to be published.

The **LOWTHER COMMITTEE** feel it their duty to disavow the publication of any hand-bills issued by **Mr. C. J. Fisher**, at Appleby, or elsewhere, as they have given no Authority whatever to **Mr. Fisher** to act on their behalf.

C. WILSON,

Chairman.

AIREY AND BELLINGHAM, PRINTERS, KENDAL.

The first Gazette Editor C. J. Fisher overreached himself. He was out of the job within seven weeks, and De Quincey was called in to harden the partisan line.

A sparkling conversationalist with a diminutive figure, Thomas De Quincey, a detail from a chalk sketch by James Archer RSA, 1855.

Draft of a letter by De Quincey that explains how he came to be Editor of the Gazette. His predecessor C. J. Fisher "disgusted" the proprietors.

means of winning notice from those learned bodies. The editor
can assure his readers that it has such means within its
certain reach. His own personal friends in most of the Universi-
-ties, especially in the three weightiest — Oxford, Cambridge,
and Edinburgh, are quite competent in num-
-ber and power to float the Gazette triumphantly into every
section and division of those learned bodies: the paper
would thus be put upon its trial: and, what would be the issue,
he cannot permit himself to doubt, — when he adds that each
and all of these friends are ready to furnish their
literary assistance in addition to that which he may
calculate upon in Westmorland. L. reminds the editor
of his 'uneducated readers' in Westmorland: the editor does not forget
them; but he is persuaded that it is a mere over-sight in L. to
have neglected mentioning his well-educated and his learned read-
-ers in the same county, who are very numerous: and from
them, also, he has reason to hope for powerful aid. He may add that, as respects this corner of the kingdom,
he has received assurances of support from two of the most illustri-
-ous men in point of intellectual pretensions that
have appeared for some ages. With such assistance,

Promises. In his draft for a Gazette article, De Quincey sets out his aim to turn the newspaper into an unrivalled literary and scientific journal.

Christopher Wilson Esq. in the Chair -
Resolved -
That Mr. De Quincey be respectfully informed that his Resignation is accepted -
Resolved.
That Mr. Kilner be for the present appointed Editor
Resolved.
That it appears advisable to this meeting that there should be a separate Establishment for the Newspaper and that the following Gentlemen be appointed a Committee to make the requisite arrangements, viz. Mr. Alderman C. Wilson, Mr. Alderman Harrison, Mr. Daniel Harrison and Mr. John Gandy -
Ordered that Mr. Kilner be instructed to make an Estimate of the necessary Types that will be wanted for a separate printing establishment and that the Committee give directions for an immediate purchase
This Meeting is adjourned to Monday se'nnight at four o'clock in the Afternoon -

Chris. Wilson

Nov. 6th 1819.

At a meeting of the Committee appointed by the Proprietors of the Westmorland Gazette to take measures to establish an independent concern & to remove the press types &c to some place which may be convenient for the purpose

Present Mr. C. Wilson
Mr. J. Harrison
Mr. D. Harrison

Mr. D. Harrison reports that he has taken rooms in the New Shambles belonging to Wm. Atkinson, Cooper, for a term of 7 years [illegible], to commence at Martinmas next, for the sum of twelve Guineas annually -

Page from the Gazette accounts book.
The end of the line for De Quincey.

Chapter Six

Newspaper at War

> *"Motion and change of scene are the life of newspaper politics: there is no unpardonable crime but tediousness; and no sin, past benefit of clergy, but dulness . . ."*
>
> *Thomas De Quincey, The Westmorland Gazette*
> *December 26th 1818.*

The first Gazette appeared under the splendid legend 'Truth we pursue, and court Decorum: What more would readers have before 'em?' It was a pithy little motto culled from Horace that was not to stay in currency very long. As the newspaper fight warmed up, each paper's correspondents cheerfully warped the unwritten rules of etiquette to suit their own political ends. But for the present, Fisher of the Gazette was a gentleman who politely pleaded that he would "offer no offence even to those from whom he may find it reasonable to differ in opinion."[1] In an effort to show how far the Chronicle had degenerated, Fisher published a prospectus identical to the one found in the first Chronicle of June 1811. Piously, and with some irony, the Gazette pronounced: "We hope that we shall never rank amongst the turbulent disturbers of public tranquillity, nor amongst the malicious enemies to domestic peace. We know that the Press may be made a great engine of evil in bad hands, but let us hope that ours will never be disgraced by the stamp of infamy."[2]

In that first Gazette issue there was little to cause offence: three columns of Parliamentary proceedings, market reports, an article about a Mayoral meeting on vagrancy, deaths, marriages, poems and a mild diatribe against Jacobinism. Fisher promised that the Gazette would be a "useful as well as an amusing companion" and he invited his readers to contribute to "fair, free but decorous discussion."[3] In short, there was little aggressive campaigning despite the imminence of the election.

However, in the next issue the Gazette produced a new pseudonymous writer, Philadelphus, whose reply to a letter in the Chronicle by slavery abolitionist Thomas Clarkson incensed the Brougham faction.

Clarkson's original letter was an elegant argument for supporting Brougham that stressed that he was an indispensable member of the Commons and suggested that the Earl of Lonsdale could easily place one of his sons elsewhere. Philadelphus commandeered the whole of the Gazette's back page to trash Clarkson's persuasive reasoning in the most witty and exhaustive fashion.

It was not exceptional for writers to guard their identity by the adoption of a pseudonym, but Philadelphus guarded his closer than most. It is only recently, in a thesis by F. S. Janzow, that a cogent argument has been put forward, firmly laying attribution for the article. Many contemporaries thought that the author may have been Wordsworth, but Janzow identifies him convincingly as De Quincey. Although final proof of authorship is unlikely to be found, Philadelphus strikes a certain De Quinceyan chord with his discursive reference to "equivocating appearances" while on the job of cutting Clarkson.

"He reminds me of children, with whom the idea of magnitude, because their pride consists in growing taller, is absorbed in the single dimension of altitude: thus, considering height alone, they are apt to call the slender, taper towering poplar bigger than the much more massy mansion near which it stands."[4]

It was not the technical mastery of language that caused a furore, but rather Philadelphus' allegation that Brougham had at one time been a spy on the Continent. As soon as Brougham arrived in Kendal on June 13th for campaigning, he responded to the libel by taking legal action against the two Gazette proprietors Thomas Maude and James Gandy (vice-president of the Lowther Committee) and also the printers, Airey and Bellingham.

Brougham used the Chronicle to refute the allegation and explain the circumstances of the spy rumour. He said that he had legitimately joined a diplomatic mission to the Portuguese Court and had then proceeded to the Court of Madrid in the hope of confirming that Spain would join the allies against Napoleon. In the event, the Prussian army was crushed by the French at the Battle of Jena and Spain got cold feet.

Despite the obvious logic in the explanation, Philadelphus had ruffled the opposition and Brougham's supporters tried unremittingly to discover his identity and discredit him. When Brougham dropped the case against the Gazette printers but pressed home with the one against the proprietors, the Secretary of the Lowther Committee and a Gazette shareholder, James Johnson, became defiant: "The proprietors are not afraid of him — and we are determined to proceed with Action upon Action against the Proprietors and Printer of the old Paper by way of retaliation."[5]

Fisher published a letter in the Gazette attacking Philadelphus for "rash and groundless assertions" though, of course, he was only living up to his promised word that opinions of both sides would find "an open stage, and fair play" in the one paper. By this time, Fisher's persistent even-handedness was beginning to worry the more passionate of the Gazette readers. One expressed disquiet about his "impartiality" and demanded assurances that although reporting would be free, full and fair, Fisher's own politics would "follow one broad straight line." The dilemma facing Fisher was highlighted in a Chronicle letter which also served as a premonition of his downfall.

"The Editor has hitherto, in a commendable manner, put in a softening word occasionally, to moderate the fury of his redoubtable correspondents. But he will presently find, that he must go all their lengths, or himself become suspected."[6]

Apart from Brougham's libel action, the other major scandal before polling involved a miscarriage in land tax assessments. Brougham said that the Clerk of the Land Tax

Commissioners, John Thompson, had put a halt on all assessments for no good reason. After weekly pleas in the Chronicle for all eligible freeholders to register in the land tax lists, Brougham interpreted the move as a deliberate attempt to stop his supporters from qualifying as voters. While the Chronicle damned the land tax manoeuvres as "the quintessence of whatever is mean and detestable, even in Toryism itself,"[7] the Gazette ridiculed the idea that any Lowther influence had been used to pressure the Clerk into his dubious decision. The Treasury said that a query had arisen over the title of a few forty shilling cottages and that the stop on assessments was limited to those in question. Lord Lowther denied all knowledge of the order, but he was finally forced to break silence when Brougham alleged that all the land tax commissioners were members of the Lowther Committee. Lord Lowther simply stated that the delay was caused by the volume of assessment claims.

While Brougham and the Lowthers battled over legalities, Wordsworth worried about possible disorder at the forthcoming polling at Appleby, and kept his master informed of local feeling.

"I believe that we are gaining ground in *many* directions —you will smile at my illustration of this, by a dialogue which took place the other day at Ambleside, between an Apothecary's apprentice and a Chimney-Sweeper's Boy. — *Boy,* 'What, you have little to do with elections here?' — *Apprentice,* 'We have had a good deal — how are they at Kendal?' — *Boy,* 'We *were* all Blues but they're turning; *My Master* promised his Vote to Brougham, but he'll give it to the Lowthers — he says, he doesn't like such black-guard work!' "[8]

Despite such reassuring news on Ambleside streetcorners, down in London the betting was all on Brougham. He had worked hard in Westmorland, often holding up to seven open air meetings a day at different venues and speaking for forty minutes at each.

Voting started on June 30th for a four day poll and, with the unfounded expectation of a full scale riot, the Lowthers made sure that the Deputy High Constable, Robert Welch, had over four hundred officers waiting at Appleby. The family also hired miners from Alston Moor and drafted in five coaches of sailors and carpenters who were all paid five shillings a day to "preserve" order. Brougham looked after the five hundred of his voters who walked the twenty-six miles from Kendal to Appleby by housing them in tents and barns along the way; and, when they arrived, the paternal Brougham complained that the armed constables and hired hands had only been recruited to intimidate his followers during hustings.

Robert Welch had proclaimed in the Gazette that his officers would show impartiality, drink not a drop of ale and wear no party ribbons. Nevertheless, he felt that his 'disinterest' deserved favour and three months after the election he applied to the Lowthers for the pay off. "The Deputy High Constable, who rendered us so much assistance at Appleby in the command of the Constables at the Election is desirous to be made Lieutenant in the Westmorland militia,"[9] Lord Lowther wrote to his father.

The election ended with 1,211 votes for Lord Lowther, 1,157 for Col. Lowther and 889 for Brougham. The land tax fiddle did not affect the result, and Brougham was easily beaten. But the Lowthers were badly shaken and while they privately resolved never to be taken by surprise again, Brougham was vowing to contest every future Westmorland election as long as he lived. Brougham announced that he was setting up a permanent county association to renew the party faith with meetings in Kendal, Appleby, Kirkby Lonsdale, Kirkby Stephen, Brough, Ambleside and Burton. He implored his members to wear blue ribbons on their arms at every public meeting and encouraged the purchase of freeholds. To prevent allegiance dying with defeat, Brougham commemorated his new association for the "independence of Westmorland" by having a special medal struck for each freeholder who had voted for him.

There was little disorder at the polls: the only injury was a head wound sustained by an innocent bystander, John Wybergh, the son of a Brougham supporter, Thomas Wybergh, of Clifton Hall. But magistrates refused to issue a warrant for the special constable who clubbed Wybergh, even though the culprit could be identified by many. Back in Kendal, a crowd assembled in front of the Commercial Inn where people fortified themselves with one hundred gallons of ale supplied by a thoughtful donor from Fell-side. The beery crew went out to greet the returning Brougham voters, and when the whole fractious mass arrived together in town, windows were broken, the Mayor called out the cavalry and finally read the Riot Act at eleven o'clock that night. The election may well have been over, but feeling was still riding high.

In early July Fisher left the Gazette, and De Quincey was asked to take over. The tables were now turned. This time De Quincey had to be asked twice whether he would take the Editor's chair, and he only consented on condition that he could continue to live at Grasmere, commute into Kendal and that a printer be hired for technical and menial work. In a letter to his uncle later that year asking for a loan, De Quincey set out the pounds, shillings and pence of his predicament.

". . . an editor was procured from London; but he disgusted them in every way and the principal gentleman of the county thus addressed an application to me — proposing that I should take the Editorship: 160£ a year was offered: but it was necessary to reside in Kendal: this I would have done but my wife's illness, and another impossibility of raising the money for removing in the time prescribed (viz. between the 9th and 16th July) obliged me at first with great pain of mind to decline it: but they then made a 2nd application — offering that a clerk of the Press should be hired to take those duties (in rt. to advertisements etc) which must be performed by someone on the spot: and that I should pay him out of the 160£ and receive the difference myself: This I accepted — the clerk was hired from a newspaper office in Manchester: he had previously 85£ per an: and he would not give up a certainty for less than 2 guineas a week: this deducted 109£. 4s. from my 160£ and left therefore but 50£. 16s. per an: however the Proprietors made it up to a guinea a week; and I have therefore a guinea a week *certain* for at least four years to come and this I can retain at any distance for, though I do now make up the Paper and select and revise all the component articles, yet this labour is no part of my duties but I have volunteered that part by way of raising the character — and extending the sale — of the Paper: but my proper duty is simply to write a political Essay on some subjects of my own choosing; and this I can do at any distance."[10]

Fisher had probably "disgusted" the Gazette proprietors for a variety of reasons. He wrote relatively timid leaders and was expensive; the Gazette accounts book reveals that he was paid off for his work on seven issues of the paper with £37 10s, and £12 12s in "extra expenses."[11] After five issues James Johnson evidently thought the paper's content was uninspired. "The Westmorland Gazette contains not much," he told the Lowthers, "but it still contains a short answer to B's late Remarks."[12] Despite De Quincey's earlier obsession to win the Editorship, he now had to be tempted into regular employment. The proprietors struck the awkward compromise by splitting his duties and allowing him to stay in Grasmere; however, these efforts to minimise the disruption to De Quincey's personal life did little to benefit the paper. The proprietors, in full knowledge, agreed to an absent Editor who would only be responsible for style, tone and literary flavour rather than decisive management of news. It was to prove a disastrous arrangement.

On the other hand, the set up suited De Quincey perfectly. He could remain in Grasmere with his beloved wife and family and write his heavily edited essays or, when he felt like it, paste up pages in the peace of his cottage. Kilner could handle all the dirty work in Kendal and be supervised on regular visits to town. The idea of an absent Editor certainly appealed because De Quincey claimed that he would be assured of his guinea a week for "at least four years" and, he boasted, "this I can retain at any distance." This probably meant that he intended to keep the job even when he resumed his law studies in London.

Wordsworth, who acted as the Gazette's unofficial executive Editor during De Quincey's brief reign, was happy to see his friend take control of the paper, and he reassured Lord

Lonsdale that the party organ was in reasonably safe hands. As ever, Wordsworth was unable to flatter without reservation.

"The Editorship of the new Kendal Paper has passed into the hands of a most able man; one of my particular Friends: but whether he is fit (I mean on the score of punctuality) for such a service, remains to be proved. His attainments and abilities are infinitely above such a station."[13]

There is no evidence to suggest that De Quincey thought his new job was demeaning in any way. His only misgiving was the temporary separation from his wife while he organised affairs in Kendal. This frustration was aggravated by dealings with the Gazette printers, which could only serve to remind him of the squabbles there had been over the publication of Wordsworth's Cintra pamphlet. In an affectionate letter to his wife, De Quincey told of his tribulations.

"I have this moment received your note. It has put me into a little better spirits; for I have been in very bad spirits ever since I left home. I quitted Grasmere with a heavy heart, and I was sure I should find nothing in Kendal to comfort me. Indeed, I have found nothing here but trouble of all sorts. I hope, however, that I shall soon get the paper into a right train; and the proprietors are very willing to allow me my own way. The trouble I find is solely among the inferior people about the press. I am truly grieved to hear of little Margaret's illness; I hope that is not the forerunner of anything worse. God bless her, poor little lamb. If you come over to-morrow in a chaise, I shall be very happy to see you; or if you prefer next week, I shall be very happy to attend you. God bless you, my sweet wife, and believe me most affectionately yours,
Thomas De Quincey."[14]

The first issue of the Gazette under De Quincey's hand was marked by a distinct change in tone and a leader that gloated over the Lowther victory. On July 11th De Quincey wrote: "In every view the contest has been of paramount rank, and by no means to be confounded with an ordinary dispute between Whig and Tory. The root and principle of the contest lay far deeper; it touched upon whatever was cardinal and of foremost concern in the frame and constitution of society. — In

Westmorland, as on a miniature stage, was rehearsed that great drama which, there is reason to fear, from this pestilent activity of the jacobinical press, and the ferocious energy of the jacobinical faction, will be one day acted, in larger proportions, upon the great theatre of the empire."[15]

The following week, on hearing of Brougham's vow that the battle had been lost but not the war, De Quincey advocated a Tory counteraction. He shrugged off any lingering complacency and, at the threat of a permanent Radical association being established in Westmorland, pursued an aggressive, partisan line. De Quincey warned his readers: "Under these circumstances it is clear that *the snake is scotched, but not killed:* the spirit of error is not dead but sleeping; and sleeping only in respect of the ultimate object proposed, but active and alive for purposes of immediate annoyance."[16]

This ferocious desire to stamp out support for Brougham stems from De Quincey's refusal to recognise the Radicals as a party, period. Unlike Wordsworth, De Quincey had never had cause to question his political beliefs; he was born into a middle class family and was a Tory by conditioning if not by instinct. De Quincey firmly believed that the glorious trinity of King, Constitution and Church was as unassailable as the symbiotic relationship of the Tories and Whigs. This two party system, he asserted, existed and thrived by virtue of the antagonistic powers acting on each other. With such effective political physics at the heart of the Constitution, De Quincey saw the Radicals only as disruptive agents determined to capsize a happy ship. The very fact that the Whigs had refused to adopt Brougham before the election was confirmation of his worst fears: the man was an outsider who wanted to break in.

"And so far from being hostile to each other, each is right only by means of and through his antagonist: for, if the Tory were not, then the Whig would be in the wrong, and so of the Tory in absence of the Whig. Taken jointly, they make up the total truth."[17]

In short, the Whigs and the Tories locked together like two hemispheres, and hence alienated any other party. De Quincey even went so far as to say that a true Tory perspective of any political question was only possible in the light of Whig opposition, and vice versa. A bunch of disaffected individuals led by "mobocrats" like Brougham represented a serious threat, not as political opposition, but as a force of disorder bearing down on the status quo of the Constitution. Such agitators had to be resisted at all cost. "The ground, the whole *arena,* is preoccupied; there is no standing room for a new party," De Quincey wrote almost twenty years after the election in his penetrating essay Toryism, Whiggism and Radicalism.[18]

De Quincey quivered with horror at proposals for extension of the franchise and most other forms of reform. He was vociferous on the failings of the Radicals who, he believed, had no coherent policy and were merely destructive, but was strangely silent on the major social ills of the day. He had little to say about the new industrial power, unemployment, poverty and the explosive growth of the cities. Hampered by such blind spots and fired with reactionary zeal, De Quincey wielded the Editor's pen.

The Gazette office was found in the centre of Kendal, on Stricklandgate, tucked between the King's Arms and the Rose and Crown Inn, more or less where the present Gazette works stand today. The premises originally belonged to William Pennington, an alderman, printer and bookseller, until 1800, when Airey and Bellingham took over as jobbing printers. Seventeen months after the first Gazette was published, the paper's proprietors bought up the printers and moved to new premises at the New Shambles, off Market Place, where an Improved Stanhope Press was installed by booksellers M. and R. Branthwaite, of Fish Market. The change of address coincided with a change of Editor: De Quincey's assistant, John Kilner, took charge in November 1819, immediately after De Quincey's resignation had been accepted by the proprietors.

The Stanhope Press was first introduced in 1800 and was based on a design, not by a printer or tradesman, but by a nobleman, the Earl of Stanhope. It retained the conventional screw of the printing press but multiplied the degree of pressure with a system of compound levers. A regulator on the upper level bar was developed to prevent this multiplication of power from damaging the press, but early models were still notoriously dangerous to operate. It seemed that some cast iron frames were simply too weak to withstand the strain. Despite such problems, the Stanhope was very popular and a great improvement on the old wooden framed press. It could produce 250 impressions an hour and print a sheet at a single pull. The Times had a "battalion"[19] of Stanhopes until 1814, and one model is reputedly still used to print bullfight posters in a Spanish town to this very day.

The charge of 7d for a Gazette included 4d stamp duty imposed on all papers. This taxation dated from 1712 when the Tory ministers of Queen Anne tried to block the opposition Press and raise extra revenue. Newspaper publishers protested for years against the 'tax on knowledge' and although the stamp was finally abolished in 1855, it had successfully choked the circulation figures of the emergent newspapers. In De Quincey's day, the paper for the Gazette was sent pre-stamped from Manchester, which, of course, made printing mistakes costly. If a sheet was spoiled, the stamp was lost.

By virtue of the stamp duty, newspapers were luxuries that only the privileged were at liberty to enjoy. The problem was partially overcome by the creation of reading rooms or coffee houses where papers would attract many readers and customers. It was a very popular idea. When men read papers, they argued, and when they argued, they became thirsty and drank plenty of coffee. The bean and print became commercial partners in the success story of the century as the number of coffee houses in London soared from a handful to over 1,600 within twenty-five years. By 1890 the Keeper of the Crown Coffee House, at Haymarket, kept his daily stream of almost 2,000 customers, from all walks of life, entertained with one of the best selection of papers and journals in the capital.[20]

In the provinces, people gathered at the best tavern, either to read the news or to have it read to them. At Kendal, the Coffee Room was established in 1779 by a club of subscribers who bought a range of newspapers and played backgammon for drinks at the White Hart. By 1804 the club had moved across the road to the Commercial Inn, subscribed to many more papers and organised opening hours from 7 a.m. to 10 p.m. During De Quincey's Editorship of the Gazette, the Coffee Room, later known as the Kendal News Room,[21] had over 100 members and many more visitors.

This was a very important readership, just across the street from the Gazette office, and De Quincey knew it well. He possessed few illusions about journalism. He was fully aware of its transient quality and the demands that such a restriction put on his writing: variety, accuracy and aggression were all vital if the paper was to capture a permanent audience. De Quincey's true aspirations were for the present postponed because, as he noted with some humour, the Gazette was hardly a passport to literary fame. In the meantime, he wanted his paper to function as a running debate, provoking and informing. There was a place for illuminating, reflective prose in the Gazette, but only if it flared like a match and burnt out just as quickly.

"A newspaper is not like a book in its duration. Books are immortal; for some of them last for ten or even fifteen years: but newspapers must content themselves with an existence almost literally ephemeral: a week is the term of their natural lives: and, if a newspaper exceeds that term, it may be said to have 'descended to posterity': the readers of the second week are the posterity of a newspaper: after which they are not much heard of except by antiquarian trunk-makers and chandlers of eminent research. — On this consideration, the Editor of a newspaper must never stop hair-splitting in defence of his logic — or apologising for his grammar and spelling. If he spells amiss one week, he must consult his spelling book and spell better the next. If the 'Chronicle' knocks the 'Gazette' down one week, the 'Gazette' must get up and knock the 'Chronicle' down the next. Motion and change of scene are the life of newspaper politics: there is no unpardonable crime but tediousness; and no sin, past benefit of clergy, but dulness . . ."[22]

Transitory things had always appealed to De Quincey by

inspiring a mixture of fear and excitement. At the Frogmore Ball as a boy, he had been moved by the fleeting nature of youth and now, as a newspaper Editor, he acknowledged the thrilling, brief life of his present labours. But this time, as the feeling of waste welled up, De Quincey did not drift into depression; he confidently grasped the challenge and strode into the ring to face the Chronicle. The newspapers were at war.

One of the first of De Quincey's editorial decisions was to abandon the usual page two general home news in favour of a bizarre story about The Incombustible Man. This was an abridgment of an article that had already appeared in The Literary Gazette and told of a man called Charbert who could chew burning coal, lick red hot pokers and bathe his feet in boiling lead without harm. Charbert was a stout fellow of Russian birth who had fallen into a fire as a child and had since been able to withstand all manner of ordeals. For those who lacked such a gift, the Gazette listed a recipe, which included marshmallow, eggs and radishes, that could be readily concocted at home for those who wanted to fireproof their own flesh. The paper did not carry any subsequent testimonials.

This esoteric selection of news sat uneasily beside De Quincey's own scholarly and allusive contributions. Oddities, such as Charbert, together with reports of murders, suicides, fires and accidents gave an inkling of De Quincey's darkest and disordered obsessions while, in contrast, his own articles showed a remarkable application of logic and organisation. It was a conflict that was never resolved, either in the newspaper or in De Quincey's life.

When the Chronicle attacked the Royal Family as pensioners on the National Bounty who cost £350,000 a year and spent most of that sum abroad, De Quincey reacted with his Defence of Royalty. "The claims of the State are peremptory and paramount, without limit, without bar, without condition,"[23] he declared. But one reader from Kirkby Thore was unconvinced. He called De Quincey's leader "a precious morsel of political chicanery," referred to the

Gazette's circulation as "notoriously very limited,"[24] and had the letter reprinted in the Chronicle. True to the promise of a blow for blow war with the Chronicle, De Quincey parried with a defence of his article that was three times longer than the original. He admitted that his writing was at least part-metaphysical and so limited his audience to an educated elite, yet he continued to defend his original article by the defined rules of scholastic logic. Having embarked on an intricate discussion, De Quincey was not going to abandon it for the sake of embracing bewildered dalesmen among his audience.

He explained and justified the four propositions: certain rights are inherent in every State and not created by any specific law; the right of taxation is one of those rights; total property of the nation belongs to the State and, if total property belongs to the State, then the State owes no gratitude to its subjects. The argument was hardline Thomas Hobbes, and De Quincey even quoted the philosopher of home peace to add weight to his article. Hobbes' analysis of power, in the light of the English Civil War, seeked to prove that taxes are payments a man must make for protection of his life and security of employment. It argued that taxes "are nothing but the Wages, due to them that hold the publique Sword, to defend private men in the exercise of severall Trades, and Callings."[25] De Quincey wholeheartedly agreed.

Wordsworth may have agreed, too, but he was more worried about the narrow appeal of the article than its intrinsic value. When he broached the subject with De Quincey, he received an astonishing reply. De Quincey apologised for his "metaphysising art" and absolved himself of editoral responsibility.

"The truth is, that it was not my doing: it was a mistake of Mr. Kilner's: I meant it to have been thrown in a corner. For I am and always have been convinced that the leading art, should be in a popular tone on a popular subject. . ."[26]

At the earliest stage of his Editorship De Quincey had insisted that he would present a "clear exposition" of leading political questions for the Westmorland yeomanry. The taxation article that alluded to Hobbes, contemporary critics of Hobbes, Thomas More and Seneca was hardly of that ilk, and it prompted Wordsworth to demand assurances that De Quincey would get back on the populist track. De Quincey's apology reveals that the absence of the Editor was already causing disruption to communications. It was simply impossible to direct a newspaper efficiently from Grasmere and, as a result, articles were postponed, submitted too late or even mislaid. De Quincey could barely keep account of the stories he wrote, never mind anyone else's, and often on arriving at the Kendal print works he found that he had not left room for the most important article of all — his. He fulfilled his need for self-justification by explaining the mismanagement in his own columns and told readers that the paper was "almost entirely pre-occupied by other matter which he had previously sent."[27] While De Quincey was juggling articles and deadlines, and occasionally fumbling both, Lord Lowther was giving Wordsworth instructions on how further opposition to Brougham should be conducted. Although the Lowthers wanted to present a united and unruffled front to Brougham, they also wanted to meet his every attack with equal force. The two strategies clashed and forced another editorial dilemma onto De Quincey.

"The Chronicle has less slander than usual and though I understand L. Thanet was most bitter and acrimonious in his speeches they affect a good humour and laugh at our wrath. It is no longer political to meet them mildly. If they recommense attacks, we must stand up to them," explained Lord Lowther, "but if they know our blood is up their behaviour will come within the circle of propriety. It is a great disadvantage to be thought proud or ill-tempered."[28]

A six installment letter under the pseudonym Philadelphus Alter was drawing to a close in the Gazette after a lengthy defence of Philadelphus. The author of this epic could well have been De Quincey because he makes an intimate defence of the motives, character and opinions of Philadelphus, who is already identified almost certainly as De Quincey. The only other possible contender, who would have had such detailed knowledge of Philadelphus (De Quincey), was Wordsworth, and it is unlikely that he would have professed to be the champion of "my persecuted friend." Persecution was De Quincey's own realm.

During this period, Wordsworth maintained a very close correspondence with Lord Lowther about the Gazette content and he followed up letters by delivering orders to De Quincey and mediating when interests conflicted. "What the Editor of the Gazette said in his last number upon this subject was not quite what I wished and we agreed upon, but I hope it would do no harm,"[29] grumbled Wordsworth in early October. The following week he noted with his usual ambivalence: "The Westnd Gazette of today has a spirited article from the Editor; a little too strong perhaps in the expression."[30]

When Wordsworth was not providing a running commentary of the Gazette content, he was trying to trace the identity of troublesome correspondents. Lord Lowther trusted him well enough to send cryptic messages such as: "The inquiry must be conducted secretly yet firmly. You know my meaning. So as soon as it could be done the better."[31] If the Gazette Editor required a chastening word, Wordsworth was the ideal messenger. Lord Lowther was determined to closely control the paper and engineer propaganda to suit the varying tone of the political battle. So, when moderation was the watchword, he secretly collected "private anecdotes" against his opponents for future use and sent his poet-agent to deal with De Quincey.

"I agree with you in my combating publick conduct and leave private scandal to the tea tables — you could instil this into the Editor though it might be improper to convey it, through any other channel but yourself,"[32] wrote Lord Lowther. Three days later Wordsworth replied dutifully: "The Editor of the Gazette is prepared to act as you wish in respect to private conduct."[33]

De Quincey was always defensive on the subject of Lowther influence. He evidently resented Wordsworth's interference and always pleaded that he wrote in complete independence. Of course, his readers were the first to hear the denial: ". . . there is no connexion subsisting between the Lowther family and the 'Gazette'. Lord Lonsdale is not a proprietor of the 'Gazette'; nor, so far as the Editor knows, is any member of his family. Whether Lord Lonsdale is even a subscriber, is more than the Editor can assert."[34]

Behind the scenes the picture was far different. In the Autumn of 1818 De Quincey ran the paper largely as he pleased while Lord Lowther exerted every available pressure in an attempt to bring him to heel. De Quincey breezily went about business as usual and let Wordsworth take most of the flak from his exasperated Lordship.

"I wish you could make the Editor superintend and do not let us place the Enemy on the advantage ground of good breeding — I am half determined never to look at another of the papers again — at all fronts it is once more troubling to you. So do pray go request the Editor to be a little more mild in his importunities."[35]

In fact, the real thorn in Lowther's side was John Fleming, the Gazette proprietor and a wounded veteran of the Kendal Riots, who embarked on a nine week serial of abuse of Brougham, which embarrassed the Lowthers and also lumbered De Quincey with accusations of lax Editorship. Lord Lowther wanted De Quincey to ditch most of the letters and fill the Gazette with abstracts from the London papers. "Really if he puts in all that is sent to him," he complained, "every clergyman and schoolmaster in the country will become an author."[36] The Gazette was branded "scurrilous and abusive," and Lord Lowther told Wordsworth that he was ashamed of the "coarse epithets applied by our friends to the motions and actions of our opponents." He was so angry when he wrote the letter that he missed out the word "friends" and only added it later.

But the solution was not simple. John Fleming, as Wordsworth argued, was upright, fiercely loyal to the Lowthers and quick to take offence. It was extremely difficult for De Quincey to cut the correspondence of one of the Gazette proprietors without adequate reason. If De Quincey did reject Fleming's letter it would only cause a breach and might even jeopardise his employment as Editor. By December, Wordsworth was despairing: "I begged him (De Quincey) to announce his determination not to tolerate long winded controversies . . . I fear the Gazette is sinking."[37]

Meanwhile, De Quincy weathered the storm by "writing in a situation of deep seclusion, and at a distance of eighteen miles from any town."[38] In other words, he was in Grasmere, dosing himself heavily with opium in the peace of his family's cottage. By now, his readers were used to his confessions and in November the paper declared: "The Editor of the Westmorland Gazette has to lament that a painful indisposition for some weeks past, which has made the act of composition very distressing to him, has prevented him from fulfilling many engagements . . ."[39]

The crazy dreams of spinning architecture climbing inestimable heights had now been replaced by visions of "lakes and silvery expanses of water," which caused headaches for two months. The waters gradually changed from shining mirrors to rolling oceans on which bobbed a new driftwood terror — "faces that surged upwards by thousands, by myriads, by generations: infinite was my agitation; my mind tossed, as it seemed, upon the billowy ocean, and weltered upon the weltering of waves."[40]

In the same month of suffering, De Quincey delivered an abstract of three reports about the funeral of Queen Charlotte, the Consort of George III. Alongside the story, his editorial attacked the treatment the event had received in the national "jacobinical press" with violence and disgust. De Quincey was depressed, sickening and sickened. He was beginning to despise his professional peers.

"In general the editors of newspapers are low-bred mercenary adventurers, without manners, without previous education, and apparently without conscience, or moral principle. They are servile to the public feeling, according to their conception of it; and that conception is derived from their own experience of life, lying originally among the needy and discontented; — not seldom from a constitution of mind predisposing them to meanness and ignoble sentiments, and from habits and education tending to confirm it."[41]

Years later, in the coolness of retrospect, the loathing resolved into pity; pity for budding talent corrupted by the constraints of journalism. De Quincey saw the young and gifted chase a craft that sucked their talent and narrowed their vision to the mill of immediate consumption. In this, De Quincey probably mourned his own fate as a writer sentenced to fritter away his time and energies in the periodical press, and even then failing to provide for his family and avoid the bailiffs. But where literature starved, De Quincey observed, journalism flourished. "Never amongst men has there been an exhibition of so much energy, vigilance, sagacity, perseverance as we of this day behold in our political press,"[42] he wrote in 1835. This was not a complete change of heart. De Quincey still felt that honour and good feeling flagged behind ability in the race for stories. However, the problem was not home grown, he asserted; it stemmed from a "spirit of violence and brutality," the first of many cultural imports from America.

The Chronicle reacted sharply to De Quincey's observations on newspaper editors and it took him to task for his snobbishness, his alleged post as "a retainer of the aristocracy" and, more truthfully, his "promising much and doing nothing." In a reply that occupied most of page three, De Quincey dealt with the criticism in his usual, discursive and self-justifying style. He had genuinely not meant to offend the Chronicle Editor and, as a proud product of the middle classes, was wary of elevating himself above his station.

De Quincey mismanaged the news because he was hypersensitive and had an irrepressible need to point out other people's errors of logic. When he did occasionally cobble together a story, De Quincey thought that his readers failed to appreciate the feast he had so carefully laid before them. He scolded them and, when they still failed to court him, he was hurt. In exasperation he held himself up for judgement and told his readers that the account of the Queen's funeral "had cost the Editor a whole day's labor — with no reward in prospect beyond the hope of furnishing an interesting subject or reading for one winter's evening to the cottagers of Westmorland."[43] The patrician's pen wept tears, not hard ink.

By the end of 1818 Fleming's series of embarrassing letters tailed off and the author was encouraged by Wordsworth to put any subsequent thoughts in a pamphlet instead of the

Gazette. As the New Year dawned, De Quincey was morose. Absorbed in personal problems, he washed his hands of troublemakers like Fleming with a whimsical editorial: "The Editor of the 'Gazette' differs in many points from many of his correspondents, in some respects perhaps from all."[44] But De Quincey emerged from this winter of opium and the threat of the debtors' prison with a renewed strength, an unexpected enthusiasm and, on a more practical level, a loan from his Uncle Penson.

John Wilson, in Edinburgh with Blackwood's Magazine, sent De Quincey a copy of David Ricardo's Principles of Political Economy and Taxation to review. The article was never written, but Ricardo's idea of economics as science was a revelation to the Gazette Editor. No sooner had he read the first chapter than De Quincey declared: "Thou art the man!"[45]

Ricardo was a successful member of the Stock Exchange who had amassed such a fortune by 1815 that he could retire at the age of forty-three. He turned writer and politician, and entered Parliament in 1819 for Portarlington, armed with an unrivalled grasp of economic theory. His Principles of Political Economy set out laws that determined the distribution of goods through the "three classes of the community": labourers, farmers and landlords. Ricardo found that the amount of labour required in the production of goods dominated their value, but did not wholly determine it. His conclusions were that profits varied inversely with wages; rent increased in relation to population growth and that overseas trade was not dominated by respective production costs, but by the internal price structures of each country. These ideas, said De Quincey, "first shot arrowy light into dark chaos of materials."[46] However, it was not so much the conclusions that so impressed the Gazette Editor, rather it was how the author had arrived at them. Ricardo had avoided the mire of facts and details that, De Quincey said, had defeated previous writers, and had rejected empirical findings in favour of a priori reasoning. De Quincey was astonished that a worthy successor to Kant had been produced in the rough and tumble of the market place instead of the academic sanctuary of Europe's universities: it was like a mongrel winning over pure breds. Despite Ricardo's lack of educational pedigree — he entered his father's business at fourteen — De Quincey adopted him as his new hero and promoted his principles whenever possible. De Quincey even said that he wrote his own Prolegomena to all Future Systems of Political Economy, dedicated to Ricardo, and engaged a Kendal printer to publish it. But he found himself "quite unable to accomplish all this"[47] and left his draft to rest, unread, alongside Ricardo's work on a Town End bookshelf. In reality, it is unlikely that De Quincey's idea for a book progressed further than an unfertilised seed and, for the present, he was content to write dissertations for the Gazette on the Bullion Question.

Ricardo's treatise The High Price of Bullion, a Proof of the Depreciation of Bank Notes had led, indirectly, to the setting up in 1810 of a special Commons' committee to report on the high price of bullion and the general state of the exchange. Under the financial strain of the war with France, the Government had forbidden the Bank of England to pay its notes in gold, under the Bank Restriction Act. This meant that the banks could increase note issue and volume of lending. However, such inflationary measures caused high prices, a fall in the foreign exchange rate and bullion to be sold over mint price.

The Bullion Committee reported that the value of paper money could only be maintained as long as it was immediately convertible into gold. It warned of the dangers of inflation and pointed to the over-issue of bank notes as the cause of the high price of bullion. Its recommendation to repeal the suspension of cash payments was unpopular with the banks and the government, and was ignored until 1821.

While the findings of the committee confirmed Ricardo's views, De Quincey remained unconvinced. In a series of articles between February and May in the Gazette, De Quincey argued the case against the resumption of cash payments in long, lucid expositions. Although he differed from Ricardo on this question, he privately acknowledged a great intellectual debt to the man. Even Gazette readers identified that the

Editor was a close student of Ricardo, though publicly De Quincey wanted to play down the connexion.

"Any such coincidence will shew itself in all probability, from the different mode of illustration, to be purely accidental: at all events, we assure the reader that — having been out of the way of all towns and libraries for some years except our very own small one — we have had no opportunity to profit by Mr. Ricardo's book, and regret that we have not —"[48]

This was probably a reference to Ricardo's High Price of Bullion, which De Quincey may well not have read. But he made up for the loss by immersing himself in his copy of Political Economy.

De Quincey's articles that dominated the Gazette during those early months of 1819 drew on the principle that metallic currency was not the best measure of national wealth. "We all know that 27 shillings could be had for a guinea: but who ever heard of any man taking or offering 18 shillings for a bank-note? Yet, according to all precedent, this should have been the form of the depreciation,"[49] he told his readers in April. He styled his discussion on the format set by Coleridge, and took every available road and lane before resuming the essential journey. "Now then let us pull up; and wheel round from this long digression into the high road of the argument,"[50] he explained in part two of Paper of the Bank of England.

His conclusion on the question of suspension of cash payments was in fierce opposition to the Commons' Committee: "The Anti-Restrictionists suppose that the Mint price of gold is the natural price, and the market price is the artificial price. The converse of this proposition, which is obviously the truth, is a talisman which disperses the whole fabric of their system into air."[51] De Quincey's interpretation of 'market value' was later revised, and in his essay the Logic of Political Economy, of 1844, he argued that true market value was set by two forces — past experience of prices and the price in relation to supply and demand. However, in 1819 he was passionately in favour of the sole rule of the market place.

Lord Lonsdale was pleased with the Gazette's support of the Government on the Bullion Question. Earlier disagreements seemed forgotten as his Lordship now tried to engineer an introduction to the Quarterly Review for De Quincey. Wordsworth thought this to be an admirable idea; but although he supported the launch of De Quincey into the national Press, he knew that the Review backed the Commons' Committee report and would probably reject any contrary view. "This I am sorry for," Wordsworth wrote, "because if De Quincey could bring his reasonings before the public through a favourable channel I think he would go far towards exploding a mischievous error."[52]

In one of De Quincey's characteristic editorials, which explicitly spelt out his personal circumstances, he excused his neglect of the Gazette and explained that he had other commitments bidding for his time. Two periodicals, "one of very great, the other of unrivalled circulation," had accepted him six months previously as a freelance writer.

"For half a year and upwards he neglected these engagements in order to give up a greater share of his time to the 'Gazette'," wrote De Quincey, "but it may be supposed that industry thrown into a national channel will be more productive than it can be when exerted within narrower limits."[53]

The Quarterly Review had sent De Quincey the works of Schiller for review, but had received no copy four months later, and had rejected all his essays on economics. Blackwood's Magazine may have been open to him for sixty guineas' worth of articles a year, but De Quincey had yet to contribute. Even though he deluded himself about his literary output, the editorial showed that De Quincey was becoming a little bored by the parochial nature of a county newspaper and was looking for fresh, more extensive, pastures.

While waiting to break out of the Gazette, De Quincey contented himself by writing hardline Tory commentary on controversies such as Catholic emancipation. His uncompromising opinion on this question, as the former Gazette Editor Charles Pollitt noted, "cannot be unearthed with any degree of credit to his genius, his political prescience, or his political charity."[54] But it would be wrong to omit digging up this disreputable nugget on the assumption that it was out of character.

"We are all agreed that 'persecution' and 'bigotry' are very bad things: but we deny that we persecute the Catholics by denying them certain privileges; and we deny that there is any 'bigotry' in refusing political power to the Catholics, so long as they profess civil doctrines such as they do profess. Their rights and liberties are as well secured as our own, and better than those of Protestants in any Catholic country in the world. But every State has a right to provide for its own safety by excluding those from power whose political principles are hostile to her interest."[55]

Yet even as De Quincey declaimed on national issues, he failed to temper his opinions with respect to the local situation. His greatest *faux pas* was on a subject close to the heart of Kendal — wool. In the same Gazette that De Quincey backed a 6d duty on imported wool, there was a report of a meeting of merchants and woollen manufacturers at the Commercial Inn, where a petition was drawn up against the proposed tax. Those involved in the trade locally feared that if the duty was imposed "a material branch of the Kendal trade would almost be annihilated."[56] The following week De Quincey spotted his error and said that he would have expressed his opinion "with more reserve" had he been aware of the petition. It was yet another example of the absent Editor's blissful ignorance of his paper's content.

It seems likely that Kilner, left to his own devices in Kendal, had slipped in the tax petition report and had no opportunity of briefing his Editor. This split management often resulted in glaring examples of poor judgement, which the Chronicle gaily held up for ridicule. Kilner once inserted a two sentence filler about the launch of the True Blue Schooner, which was drawn by four horses, followed by a procession of hundreds and heaved into Windermere at Low Wood to the stirring sound of a twenty-one gun salute and two bands playing Rule Britannia. It was a major event by any standards. But since it was a publicity stunt staged by Brougham, Kilner dismissed a report by three Ambleside correspondents and called the launch "an exhibition of folly and intemperance, and therefore unworthy of notice."[57] When De Quincey disavowed knowledge of Kilner's note, but also attacked those who attended the launch, the Chronicle had a field day.

"Now, Mr. Editor, what sort of man can you be to use, such public defamatory, unchristian-like language to your Father in law," raged Lough, "for your Father in law, Mr. Editor, was one of those outrageous, lawless and cowardly people — he accompanied the procession from beginning to end. . ."[58]

John Simpson was evidently no less a "rank Jacobin" than he had been before his son-in-law took up the Gazette Editorship. On pinpointing De Quincey's weakness, the Chronicle came in for the kill with some reflections on the Editor's own eccentricities. "During the year you have lived in this neighbourhood," it queried, "did you ever receive the least insult or injury even in your midnight rambles through and around this town . . . from any one of us?"[59]

De Quincey was mortified at Kilner's presumption and the advantage laid at the Chronicle's feet. Once again it was a vexation he could well do without. He complained to Wordsworth: "How can we expect to be furnished with true accounts of things, — or that the enthusiasm of the party should be maintained, if an ignorant lad who is perhaps making love to a blue girl shall be permitted to stifle the representations of three correspondents at once?"[60]

By the summer of 1819 De Quincey was fast losing interest in the Gazette and all the associated problems of administration, consistency and the pettish exchange between rival papers. One of his final political articles, noteworthy for its stance rather than expression, is an exoneration of the magistrates who gave the order to dissolve the reform meeting at St. Peter's Field, Manchester, which resulted in eleven killed and four hundred injured.

The Peterloo Massacre was a great blunder by the authorities, who dealt with an explosive situation without a fleeting thought for tact. Over 80,000 people gathered at St. Peter's Field on August 16th to hear the firebrand Radical 'Orator' Hunt. The meeting was legal, but the magistrates sent in constables escorted by the Manchester Yeomanry to arrest Hunt only minutes after he had begun to speak. The error lay in the decision to send in the yeomanry, who lacked proper military training and were drawn mainly from the employers' class; of course, most of those on the field to hear Hunt were employees. The class tension that had simmered for months erupted in violence and in the ensuing riot regular troops were summoned to clear the field. Many people were ridden down or crushed in the panic, mainly because some exits from the field were closed.

Hunt was sentenced to two years in prison and the Manchester Yeomanry were congratulated on a job well done by the Home Secretary, Viscount Sidmouth. Outrage swept through the country, and later that year the Government imposed the Six Acts to deal with the discontent that had spread through the lower orders.

In Kendal, the Chronicle promoted a fund for the families of the bereaved while the Gazette argued that it had been the magistrates' duty to dissolve the meeting. "Never yet indeed, since there were mobs to be controlled and laws to control them in England," wrote De Quincey, "never yet (we will venture to say) did any magistrate cause the riot act to be read — but that some were found to complain of it as an unnecessary precaution."[61]

Southey agreed with De Quincey and, in a letter printed in the Gazette, he explained that the principle was not whether the magistrates had used the correct means to break up the meeting, but whether they were allowed by law to intervene before the crowd rioted of its own accord. He argued that the question people should have been asking was whether such meetings could ever be held without endangering "not only tranquillity and safety alone, but the very existence of the country."[62]

But however faithfully De Quincey and his friends played the Tory line in the pages of the Gazette, partisanship could not dispel the problems caused by ineffective management. The proprietors realised their mistake of letting the Editor conduct business from Grasmere, and on June 29th they sent him a memorandum that asked him to tighten up the supervision of news and also directly criticised his handling of the political rivalry. The Gazette accounts book reads:

"That a notification be made to the Editor expressing their sentiments of the great importance of a regular communication between the Editor and the printer of The Westmorland Gazette, by want of which it appears that great inconvenience has frequently arisen from the exclusion of the latest London News; and the Committee trust that the Editor will take effectual measures in future to prevent a recurrence of that inconvenience which they conceive has arisen from his residing at so great a distance from the office.

"They also beg leave to suggest to the Editor the propriety of abstaining from direct remarks on any productions or observations which may appear in the Kendal Chronicle."[63]

The Committee resolved to hold another meeting as soon as De Quincey replied. It met again on November 5th to accept his resignation; so evidently De Quincey had been in no hurry to reply. Kilner became Editor and a special sub-committee was formed to organise the transfer of the print-works to the New Shambles. The following month, the rival Editor, Lough, resigned and, according to Wordsworth, Wakefield refused to advance any more money to the Chronicle, already heavily in debt. In contrast, De Quincey left the Gazette as a solvent business and as an established country newspaper. However, after his departure shareholders did not see another dividend for at least seven years. In 1824 Lord Lowther wanted to "smother" the Gazette, and two years later the situation had still not improved. "We distribute some newspapers about election time," wrote Lord Lowther, "but we can never do enough ourselves to raise a sale sufficient to make it profitable."[64]

De Quincey had pushed the Gazette out to the farthest corners of the county where it had threatened other journals. But under subsequent "indifferent" Editorship, the paper lost its advantage. Gone were the days when Wordsworth could boast to the Lowthers: "A late Clerk of the Proprietor of the Whitehaven Gazette told Mr. De Quincey that his master had lost a great part of his business since he engaged in that undertaking."[65] Such a testimonial is proof that De Quincey had faithfully practised Daniel Stuart's dictum that the first priority of the paper was to secure occupation of a large circulation area. As for the Kendal newspaper war, that continued to rage without the help of either Lough or De Quincey. James Johnson was still complaining about the "rivals in scurrility and personal abuse"[66] in 1822, and pondering on yet another change of Editor at the Gazette.

Contrary to the generally accepted myth of De Quincey as a hectoring journalist in his drugged days at the Gazette, he was a polite, if over-wrought writer who merely failed to control his "old bachelor preciseness." Errors of any sort offended him and he corrected them all at painstaking length. It was this relentless quest to put people right that sparked off the folklore of De Quincey's love of abuse; in fact, he hated the scrabbling slanging and it was probably a major reason for his leaving. The real culprits were the Gazette correspondents who raked the coals of ill-temper while De Quincey did what he could to placate the proprietors and Wordsworth, yet ended up failing in the eyes of all. De Quincey resented the Lowther pressure and always resisted. The county family wanted a veto on virtually everything to do with politics, but De Quincey did not oblige. Lord Lowther said that he thought it "but reasonable that any thing that is published under the shape of authority, should first be submitted to Henry and myself."[67] In this way the family had hoped to "guard against the zeal" of its friends, particularly against the "useless and unnecessary fire"[68] of John Fleming. De Quincey wanted to guard against the fire of Fleming, too, but he did not care to bow to all the Lowther orders. He struggled with this dilemma and managed to maintain an editorial independence that was soon lost after his resignation; for example, in early February 1820 Lord Lonsdale knew exactly what stories would appear in the next issue. Keeping the Lowthers at bay had been no mean feat, especially for a man whose very will was sapped by drug addiction.

"The opium-eater loses none of his moral sensibilities or

aspirations; he wishes and longs as earnestly as ever to realise what he believes possible, and feels to be exacted by duty; but his intellectual apprehension of what is possible infinitely outruns his power, not of execution only, but even of proposing or willing."[69]

This slow corrosion of will, revealed in De Quincey's slipshod management of the Gazette, was wedded to a more elaborate and chilling distortion of his personality which, in turn, influenced his journalism and selections of news. The fillers and features, murders and miracles, which were grafted out onto the Gazette from London papers, gave a valuable outlet to a mind tormented by nightmares. A psychiatrist might even have called the exercise therapeutic.

Chapter Seven

The Babbling Garrulity of Daylight

"How general is that sensuous dulness, that deafness of the heart, which the Scriptures attribute to human beings."
Thomas De Quincey, Masson X, 101.

Like most provincial papers, the Gazette used other journals as a free news service and snipped out interesting titbits for its own pages. De Quincey's distinction from fellow Editors was that he selected items by following his own roving whim for the eccentric, bizarre and macabre. By chance, the curiosities that he plucked from the pages of any journal, from the Literary Gazette to the German Pedagogic Magazine, seemed to appeal equally to many of his readers. This was no surprise to De Quincey who merely assumed that his taste would match everyone else's. He rooted out aberration, invention, abnormality and any event that exposed life as raw and thrilling. These criteria for the selection of news may be little different to those successfully applied in some of our contemporary national newspapers, but they run contrary to the philosophy of the local Press. The record of ordinary county happenings was included in the Gazette, but more often than not it was abandoned in favour of Assize reports of gory deeds or some peculiar abstraction such as Habits of the Orang-Outang, which was unlikely to serve any local community except a native village in Borneo. Yet, however careless De Quincey may have been of local affairs outside politics, he managed to transform the Gazette with his punctilious prose into one of the most literary papers in the provinces. No other could boast an Editor of such erudition and perception. A rare glimpse of the man at work as he cast his eye over publications to be gutted, filleted and discarded, is revealed in the one instance when he appeared in the news himself.

"On Thursday night, January 28, an accident occurred at the house of Mr. De Quincey in Grasmere, which providentially terminated without injury to any of the family. Between one and two o'clock Mr. De Quincey was sitting up writing: in a single moment a volume of smoke passed between him and his paper so suddenly as to darken it in one instant as much as if candles had been extinguished. On looking round to the fire, nothing was at first seen; but in half a minute a great fork of flames, extending to a place about four feet distant, sprung out from a crevice on one side of the grate. The rest of the family, who were then asleep, were called up; and though only women, showed so much presence of mind — that in half an hour (water being at hand) the fire was extinguished . . . The family were thankful, that one of their number was sitting up: for within half an inch of the place whence the first flames sprang out, and separated only by the side of a bookcase, stood a collection of books; and, the room being strewed on that evening with newspapers, and the timbers of the house all old, there was little doubt that in ten minutes the fire would have been inextinguishable in a place so remote from fire engines . . ."[1]

The scene is graphic. De Quincey was working in the early hours of the morning, fishing stories from a mess of papers in the desperate hope of filling the Gazette columns for Friday, press day. With so much kindling strewn about the floor of Town End, the family was indeed lucky to escape alive. Even the Chronicle, in a rare moment of conciliation, congratulated De Quincey on his good fortune in rescuing his family from "one of the most terrible of human calamities."[2]

The job of collecting stories was, according to De Quincey, Kilner's responsibility. However, although De Quincey thought himself best qualified to cater solely for the learned strata of Westmorland readership, he often assumed the duty of sifting through the London papers at Grasmere. "I had during the week compelled myself to make up the Paper," he told Wordsworth in September 1818, "nearly the whole was of my selection."[3] De Quincey achieved great success with his compilations of 'shorts' and each week the Gazette's story count far exceeded that of the Chronicle's — on average by thirty per cent. This was no accident. De Quincey realised that, on the whole, readers were lazy and wanted tempting morsels rather than indigestible gobbets of information.

"If he that writes a column have a hundred readers, he that writes two columns must possibly be content with the square root of that number: whilst he that limits himself to a quarter of a column may hope for readers that will be the biquadrate of the first. The glory will be the same proportion . . ."[4]

De Quincey took the job of lifting stories very seriously, and he despised Editors who avoided "the fatigue of hunting for articles of greater amusement."[5] He did not simply cut stories out and pack them off to Ambleside for the mail coach to Kendal. When the item was of importance or lengthy he wrote his own version in the form of an abstract to render the article "more luminously" to readers. Within a few weeks of becoming Editor, De Quincey presented his first example of a digest, the trial of Hussey. He allowed such court reports "presidency of all other news" for three express reasons: "First, Because to all ranks alike they possess a powerful and commanding interest . . . Secondly, Because to the most uneducated classes they yield a singular benefit by teaching them their social duties in the most impressive shape . . . Thirdly, Because they present the best indication of the moral condition of society . . ."[6]

De Quincey ripped the original story apart and started from scratch by working the evidence of the complicated Hussey case into two sections. Circumstantial evidence was unravelled and presented again in more palatable form, a task which De Quincey called "elaborate analysis." This self-inflicted chore was just the sort of mental gymnastics that De Quincey enjoyed, but it was not an achievement that was likely to draw acclaim from his readers. So although De Quincey gave his virtuoso pieces a grand build-up, the reception was usually disappointing. On finding that appreciation was negligible, De Quincey pushed his readers to compare his work with the original so that they would "see cause to give him credit for severe accuracy and for zeal in the service of the public."[7] This was a peculiar request and one which could only have come from a man who was desperate for approval. It was as if De Quincey was back in the Rev. Hall's class, under the regime of sermon learning and Monday tests. As a child he had feared the drudgery of memorising the minister's words; but now he refined that labour into an uncommon talent for precis, a love of logic's beautiful simplicity and a need to feel that it was all worthwhile.

Towards the end of 1818 De Quincey finally realised that he would win no medals for his endeavours. Even the Chronicle correspondents were bemused by the Gazette's rather pious delivery of the goods. "I have seen a drowned rat abstracted from immersion," wrote one, "but never heard before of a creature or thing immersed in abstractions."[8]

De Quincey threw in the towel. He was hurt by the lack of interest and mortified by ridicule. As he petulantly declared an end to his abstracts, he did not miss one last chance of explaining how dear they had cost him.

"This is a labour of the most unpretending rank. It is however far more fatiguing, more expensive of time, and more trying to the patience, than an equal quantity of original composition. In the conduct of this paper there has been hitherto much latent labour of this kind wholly thrown away: it has not merely been a thankless labour; but in far the greater number of cases has probably not been even observed."[9]

Though De Quincey was all too aware of the invisibility of his abstracting work, he still continued the practice into 1819. Perhaps it was a habit ingrained so deeply by the Rev. Hall that De Quincey found himself in an involuntary pursuit of compression, clarification and the praise that he had never been granted. This obsession did him no harm in the long term and exerted a major influence on his style of periodical journalism.

The selection and delectation of Assize reports led, most

probably, to comparison of respective crimes. Which had the most unusual twists? Which gave new insight into the mind of the criminal? The abstraction of cases put De Quincey in the position of a demi-god; he broke down the subjects to component parts before weighing and savouring each turn of evidence. De Quincey was not so arrogant as to produce a retrial; rather he looked upon the distinctions as an exercise in aesthetics. He became a connoisseur in a speciality where there were few. "As to old women, and the mob of newspaper readers," he remarked, "they are pleased with anything, provided it is bloody enough."[10] Voyeurism satisfied the mass taste while privately De Quincey became fascinated by the psychology of the murderer. He saw little worth critical attention in the mentality of victims who, quite naturally, were reduced to the "abject and humiliating" instinct of self-preservation. It was the compulsion of the murderer that was so thrilling.

"In the murdered person, all strife of thought, all flux and reflux of passion and of purpose, are crushed by one overwhelming panic; the fear of instant death smites him 'with its petrific mace.' But in the murderer, such a murderer as a poet will condescend to, there must be raging some great storm of passion — jealousy, ambition, vengeance, hatred — which will create a hell within him; and into this hell we are to look."[11]

Four years after De Quincey gave up his Editorship, he wrote a brief essay in which he tried to define the act of murder in terms of mood and omen, using a dramatic highlight from Shakespeare as a starting point. It was familiar ground. De Quincey was investigating how external influences affected sensibilities. Called On Knocking at the Gate in 'Macbeth', and published in the London Magazine, the celebrated essay explored a new field in literary criticism and was an indirect product of De Quincey's dealings with Assize abstracts at the Gazette.

"From my boyish days I had always felt a great perplexity on one point in *Macbeth.* It was this: The knocking at the gate which succeeds to the murder of Duncan produced to my feelings an effect for which I could never account. The effect was that it reflected back upon the murder a peculiar awfulness and a depth of solemnity."[12]

De Quincey was astonished at freak crimes and held them up as deeds which, in the very act of taking life, define life as vital and fierce. But his emotional response to the murderer was not always one of reverence. On a less serious note, De Quincey occasionally invested his horror stories with a shot of sardonic humour. A gem he culled from a German journal told of a Stockholm labourer who buried a block of wood in his wife's coffin and used her body as a bait for wild animals. The hunter trapped a wolf and two foxes before he was caught himself, whereupon he claimed a reward for destroying dangerous beasts. Another curiosity from De Quincey's 'foreign desk' told of the trial of an African called Pei who had murdered a fellow native and eaten part of him. When asked if he 'liked' to be tried by the foreman of the jury, Pei had replied that he liked him so much that he would eat him if he could catch him. It was this streak of black humour that prefigured De Quincey's 1827 essay On Murder Considered as One of the Fine Arts, which revolved round a dinner party of the Society of Connoisseurs in Murder. Speakers toasted the exploits of the Thugs, Assassins and the Jewish Sicarii, whose speciality was stabbing people in the pressure and secrecy of crowds. The guest lecturer told the assembly: "People will begin to see that something more goes to the composition of a fine murder than two blockheads to kill and be killed, a knife, a purse and a dark lane. Design, gentleman, grouping, light and shade, poetry, sentiment, are now deemed indispensable to attempts of this nature."[13]

A postscript to the essay gave a full account of the Williams' murders of 1811 in which two families had been massacred. The point of interest here was that the servant who had discovered the first bloodbath had knocked on the door of the house while the murderer was still inside. It was De Quincey's Macbeth come to life. The orgy of violence had happened in a fragment of time divorced from the real world. Only when that real world encroached, after the evil deed was complete, did the full import of the events gather their terrible weight.

De Quincey readily identified this suspension at a time of acute emotional upheaval for it was an intrinsic part of his own life and had been experienced at Elizabeth's deathbed and on the evening of reflection before his flight to London.

Assize reports were not the only source of the macabre in the Gazette. Quirks of fate attracted De Quincey's eye, too. Such stories included: a repeat hanging; the corpse of a hatchet attack victim being eaten by a pet pig; an apothecary's assistant being blown up after a spark fell in his pocket of fireworks and the curious coincidence of a Kendal man who died after falling into a vat of boiling glue on the day that his young son drank water from a boiling kettle. De Quincey loved focusing on the moment of crisis; for example, when the apothecary's lad made his dread discovery.

"The boy was terrified, and did not put his hand into his pocket for fear of burning it; in vain did he call bystanders, for they were equally terrified with himself. Shortly, a tremendous explosion was heard, and the spectators were shocked by the horrible sight of his bowels gushing from his abdomen."[14]

In the case of the repeat hanging, the rope broke when the trapdoor flew open and the Dublin criminal fell twelve feet onto a stone floor. He was put out of the misery of his injuries by being dusted down, carried back up to the scaffold and hanged properly.

Suicides were also attractive. De Quincey published individual cases and gave background in the form of obscure statistics of suicides for every town in Prussia. There was the tale of a well-dressed stranger who had walked into a barber's and, instead of a shave, had asked for his throat to be cut. And there was a man who had jumped out of a window after cutting his own throat: "It appears that after he cut his throat, he cut a deep wound in his side, and having opened the razor he thrust it into the aperture, which closed up, and when he was taken to the Hospital, the wound was sewed up by the surgeon, not supposing anything was in the inside."[15]

De Quincey's finest excursion into the revelation of pure physicality was the feature called Galvanic Experiments on the Dead Body of a Murderer. Only months after publication of

Mary Shelley's melodrama Frankenstein, the Gazette Editor gave his readers details of the experiments of Dr. Ure, of Glasgow, who used electric rods to contract muscles on the corpse of a thirty-year-old murderer.

"On moving the second rod from the hip to the heel, the knee being previously bent, the leg was thrown out with such violence as nearly to overturn one of the assistants, who in vain attempted to prevent its extension . . . Every muscle in his countenance was simultaneously thrown into fearful action; rage, horror, despair, anguish, and ghastly smiles, united their hideous expression in the murderer's face, surpassing for the wildest representations of a Fuseli, or a Kean. At this period several of the spectators were forced to leave the apartment from terror or sickness, and one gentleman fainted . . ."[16]

This was dangerous ground for someone who was already haunted by a sea of faces in his drug reveries. Once again, De Quincey found himself chasing things that offered an element of terror. Galvanic experiments were novel, their potential unknown. Dr. Ure pronounced that, but for the incisions into the blood vessels and spine of the murderer, life could have been restored. So who was De Quincey not to believe him?

Laudanum was never far from De Quincey's hand or mind. When the Gazette Editor was not drinking his potion, he was selecting articles about it. He told the sad tale of the wife of the Rector of Llanfaelog, at Anglesey, who by mistake took a draught of laudanum instead of her correct medicine, and died within a few hours, leaving a family of nine children.[17] In a similar case, when an eighteen-year-old Whitehaven girl went to buy aloes for a bowel complaint but instead was given a fatal dose of opium, De Quincey headlined the story 'Caution to Druggists.' But, of course, opium was not all bad news. Although it was the overdose favoured by suicidal, spurned lovers — probably because it was the most easily available drug — opium promised medicinal use. De Quincey related how a woman, whose dress caught fire after she had pressed coals onto a grate with her foot, lived for two hours while her family "administered nothing but laudanum to relieve her pains."[18] The only example of opium actually curing an ailment was an unlikely story about the dosing of a kennel of hounds suspected of rabies. It was a classic De Quincey: incredible yet logical, persuasive and whimsical.

". . . he administered opium in such large doses that some of the dogs slept almost constantly for the space of twenty-one and even twenty-eight days. The result however justified the hypothesis and the practice grounded upon it; for the whole kennel recovered their health and did not afterwards experience any relapse."[19]

Having recently been bitten three times in succession by a dog, De Quincey was not one to overlook the moral of the tale. Laudanum was certainly an exhilarating protection against rabies and, judging from the plethora of Gazette reports of dog attacks, there were plenty of other people who would have benefitted from a draught of De Quincey's ruby ruin. After his experience with vicious dogs, the Gazette Editor published every story about rabies that he could lay his hands on. Whether he collected them out of morbid self-interest or as a public warning is uncertain; however, he did reprint a letter from The Times advocating muzzling and he also appealed for better control of dogs in Sheffield. As a confirmed hypochondriac for whom rabies was the ultimate fear, De Quincey loved scaring himself by noting that each death "shows how lamentably distant we are from anything like a cure."[20] He lingered over descriptions of hydrophobic death spasms as if to reassure himself of the awfulness of such an end. The most eloquent account of this hideous death concerned John Leadbeater, unfortunate resident of that dog infested town, Sheffield.

"He seemed to die by too rapid a combustion of life, as if the that in the course of nature might have warmed and cheered existence for forty years to come, had all been condensed and expended in the space of two days; sensibility being so quickened that a drop of liquid was as difficult to swallow as the ocean, and a breath of air as terrible as a blast of Simoon."[21]

Although the conclusion of most rabies stories was inevitable, De Quincey produced one that ended on a more optimistic note. He found a tale in a German newspaper that told of a seven-year-old boy from Weser who had saved his sister from a mad dog by wrapping a coat round his arm as bait. It was a marked contrast to De Quincey's own childhood experience of a rabid dog, when his brother had goaded the mad beast and beckoned it to attack — out of fun.

Memories of early life played as large a part in De Quincey's selection of news as his current experience. He never forgot the injustice of being swiped by a teacher, an act which cut short his career at Bath Grammar School, or the cruelties that drove Pink to run away to sea. With these resentments in mind he discovered a story in the German Pedagogic Magazine about a master who multiplied the horror a hundredfold. An usher at a Spanish School, ruled with "old fashioned severity," recalled that one master had given 911,500 canings and 124,000 floggings within the span of a fifty-one year tyranny.

"It was further calculated, that he made 700 boys *stand on peas,* 600 *kneel on the sharp edge of wood,* 5,000 wear the fool's cap and 1,700 hold the rod. How vast is the quantity of human misery inflicted by a single perverse educator. But we are growing more humane, as Martial says, Ferulae tristes, sceptia paedagogorum, sessent."[22]

De Quincey always held that his variety of youthful experience had prepared him well for his job at the Gazette, and he was not shy about declaring his advantage. "The Editor has had an opportunity from his earliest youth," he told his readers, "of mixing freely in all ranks of society to that extent which he has declared necessary for a political author."[23] De Quincey had met King George III and had mingled with prostitutes; the latter was the more formative of the two experiences, though how it had affected his reactionary political outlook is anyone's guess. Ann of Oxford Street, the girl who had saved De Quincey from the London gutters and was now idealised in his reveries, crept into his life again by proxy. The pangs of regret and remorse over her loss must have stabbed sharply when this new waif was discovered.

"*Early Depravity* — A girl, (apparently *not more than twelve years old),* was brought up, being found about four o'clock, lying in the street at Whitehall. She said she had absconded from her father, a corn-chandler at Putney, in June last; that ever since she had been in the most wretched state of prostitution, generally sleeping in the park. She was covered with rags."[24]

The girl was also evocative of the nameless orphan who had crept sadly about the cold, unfurnished rooms of the money lender Brunell when De Quincey was waiting for a loan. The memories were inescapable. Images of the strays he had left behind him returned like ghosts, and when they were not actively part of his reveries, they stood silently offstage awaiting cue. Fears of the exotic and alien then mingled with these memories to produce a stream of opium invention.

Once, De Quincey looked up from his books to see a Malay, dressed in baggy white trousers and turban, standing in the kitchen at Town End. After being struck by the contrast of the "exquisite bloom" of his maidservant's complexion next to the "sallow and bilious" skin of the Malay, De Quincey tried a few languages by way of introduction. He knew one word of Turkish — 'madjoon,' meaning opium — and ended up chatting in Greek. With conversation in short supply, De Quincey offered the fierce looking stranger hospitality in the form of a chunk of opium cut in three pieces that was sufficient to "kill some half-dozen dragoons, together with their horses."[25] The Malay swallowed it at one mouthful, rested a while and then resumed his journey, probably to the seaport of Whitehaven or Workington. After that weird encounter, the Malay fastened upon De Quincey's fancy and "ran a-muck" in dreams flooded with Asiatic and Oriental scenery.

De Quincey unearthed fresh, exotic terrors in Alexander von Humboldt and Aimé Bonpland's account of expeditions in South America, which he presented as a book review in the pages of the Gazette. In 1800 Humboldt, a former Prussian mining official, had set off on a perilous five year trip to the Upper Orinoco and unknown region of the Casiquiare Canal. Along the way there had been scarcely a moment, Humboldt said, when he had not seen six crocodiles resting with gaping jaws on the riverbanks. These creatures, he noted, were excellent swimmers but had difficulty in turning about. At night the crocodiles were attracted by Humboldt's camp fire and they had ranged round it, staring at the flames for hours. This constant reptilian threat lodged in De Quincey's imagination and revived a familar torment. "The cursed crocodile became to me the object of more horror than all the rest," he wrote in his Confessions. "I was forced to live with him . . . for centuries."[26] One story of Humboldt's ordeal — a crocodile attack on a young Indian girl — especially disturbed De Quincey and, after it was published in the Gazette, its motifs returned in distorted form.

"When she felt herself seized, she sought the eyes of the animal, and plunged her fingers into them with such violence, that the pain forced the crocodile to let her loose, after having bitten off the lower part of her left arm. The girl, notwithstanding the enormous quantity of blood she lost, happily reached the shore, swimming with the hand she had still left."[27]

Thirty years later De Quincey wrote his rich, mellifluous essay celebrating, by its title, The English Mail Coach. In this work he remembers the lovely woman-child Fanny of the Bath Road, whose grandfather was a coachman and the object of outrageous speculation. De Quincey used to sit behind him on the journey, musing over his likeness to a crocodile. "This lay in a monstrous inaptitude for turning round," wrote De Quincey, "the crocodile, I presume, owes that inaptitude to the absurd *length* of his back; but in our grandpapa it arose from the absurd *breadth* of his back, combined possibly, with some growing stiffness of his legs."[28]

The association was cemented in recollection and the hunched old man became "a venerable crocodile, in a royal livery of scarlet and gold, with sixteen capes . . . driving the four-in-hand from the box of the Bath mail."[29] Even the memory of the beautiful Fanny was corrupted in the dream vision as she called up a bestial host of griffins, dragons and sphinxes into a towering "armorial shield," which was topped by a disembodied female hand pointing heavenwards. Such a stream of jumbled symbolism owes much to the account of

Humboldt's travels and particularly to the detail of the Indian girl who lost part of her arm in a crocodile attack. After all, De Quincey never forgot the things that worried him most; he cherished and revived such champions of his nightmares.

The mail coach thrilled De Quincey from boyhood through to his adult years. In the Lake District the necessity to be in two places at once meant that he and his wife were regular customers on the northbound coach from Kendal in the early hours of the morning. These journeys at "railroad pace" through the deserted villages left a profound impression on De Quincey as the "sleeping woods . . . re-echoed the uproar of trampling hoofs and groaning wheels." De Quincey and Margaret quietly held hands and looked out on the solemn, hushed hills while the coach careered homewards. "And on such nights it was no sentimental refinement," wrote De Quincey, "but a sincere and hearty feeling, that, in wheeling past the village churchyard of Staveley, something like an outrage seemed offered to the sanctity of its graves by the uproar of our career."[30]

During the summer of 1818 De Quincey made a memorable coach journey, returning from Wrington where he had been visiting his mother. This trip produced an exciting adventure which was later spun into the remarkable fantasy sequence of The English Mail Coach.

De Quincey dosed up with laudanum during a change of horses at Manchester before resuming his seat next to the driver. In the first mild hallucinations De Quincey comfortably watched the driver turn into a Cyclops, but was unnerved when the 'monster' showed a very real tendency to fall asleep. Ten miles outside Preston, De Quincey was in sole charge of the galloping London and Glasgow mail. Suddenly, as the mail dashed along a 600 yard avenue lined with trees, De Quincey spotted a young man and woman in a "frail, reedy gig" in his direct path, one and a half minutes away. He sat mesmerised at the horrific scene unfolding. The young gig driver, though, managed to slew out of danger just as the coach nicked his wheel. De Quincey was appalled: "Oh, raving of hurricanes that must have sounded in their young ears at the moment of our transit! Even in that moment the thunder of collision spoke aloud."[31]

The horror and recoil that were evoked by the narrow escape caused De Quincey to idealise the experience into a rolling succession of dreams, with freeze-frame shots of the collision course spliced between. Even during the original nightmare, De Quincey had felt impotent and oddly divorced: "The actual scene, as looked down upon from the box of the mail, was transformed into a dream as tumultuous and changing as a musical fugue."[32]

The moral inertia which had gripped De Quincey since earliest childhood found a perfect playground in this crisis of responsibility. Why had he not acted to prevent collision? The lifelong fear of the exercise of will, which had first been glimpsed in an infant's dream of a lion, now rioted. It placed the mail coach crisis on a par with the Fall from Eden and left De Quincey wracked with guilt. The snares and baits with which De Quincey had flirted throughout his life for their sparkle of terror were an apprenticeship for this one and a half minute temptation into the "luxury of ruin".

"The situation here contemplated exposes a dreadful ulcer, lurking far down in the depths of human nature. It is not that men generally are summoned to face such awful trials. But potentially, and in shadowy outline, such a trial is moving subterraneously in perhaps all men's natures. Upon the secret mirror of our dreams such a trial is darkly projected, perhaps, to every one of us. That dream, so familiar to childhood, of meeting a lion, and through languishing prostration in hope and the energies of hope, that constant sequel of lying down before the lion, publishes the secret frailty of human nature — reveals its deep-seated falsehood to itself — records its abysmal treachery. Perhaps not one of us escapes that dream . . ."[33]

Although De Quincey was never explicit about his nest of obsessions and fears during his time at the Gazette, he littered the pages of his newspaper with clues. These pointed to drug addiction, hypochondria, childhood memories, a fascination with the criminal mind and a wonder at the "colossal guilt" of the world. Deeper still, De Quincey introduced key aspects of his dream mythology and identified the "dreadful ulcer" he had discovered in human nature. In this way, an entirely innocent account of a lion hunt in India was transformed into an allegory which lifted the veil from De Quincey's private conflict over will. By such shy and circuitous means, De Quincey used the Gazette as a training ground for turning introspection into public confession.

"We now learnt, that the shot which we had heard, when down below, was occasioned by the lioness having made a spring at a poor man, who stood panic struck, unable to discharge his piece, or to run away. She had him thrown down and got him completely under her, and his turban in her mouth."[34]

De Quincey, like the Indian, often found himself panic struck, unable to exercise will one way or the other. In the most superficial sense this was revealed in his empty promises and apologies. More profoundly, he was petrified by the horror and wonder of the world. He was blinded by humanity and saw a life, a revelation and a confession in every story. He was passionate and chaotic, vulnerable and unpredictable: De Quincey was an Editor crippled by his own sensitivity because, thankfully, he never suffered from "deafness of the heart." In his own words, a newspaper exposes and yet benumbs the terrifying truth of our own lives.

"Were there no other section in it than simply that allotted to the police reports, oftentimes I stand aghast at the revelations there made of human life and the human heart — at its colossal guilt, and its colossal misery; at the suffering which oftentimes throws its shadow over palaces, and the grandeur of mute endurance which sometimes glorifies a cottage. Here transpires the dreadful truth of what is going on for ever under the thick curtains of domestic life, close behind us, and before us, and all around us. Newspapers are evanescent, and are too rapidly recurrent, and people see nothing great in what is familiar, nor can ever be trained to read the silent and the shadowy in what for the moment, is covered with the babbling garrulity of daylight."[35]

Epilogue

De Quincey achieved far more than anyone gave him credit for in his seventeen months as Editor of the Gazette. He succeeded in reshaping an ineffectual newspaper into a hardline Tory flagship, which threatened not only the Kendal Chronicle, but also papers in surrounding districts. His thorough understanding of the nature and appeal of journalism helped attract a dedicated readership and establish a sound commercial base. For all this he was given no thanks. Instead, he has only been remembered for his broken promises, his mismanagement of news, his love of Assize reports and his drug addiction. But De Quincey's guilt on all four accounts does not overshadow the fact that, at the end of the day, he left the Gazette in better standing than it would be found nearly ten years after his resignation. Sadly, the legend of the Opium-Eater, which De Quincey himself so eagerly cultivated, has eclipsed such detail.

De Quincey's own expectations for the Gazette, outside political duty and general news, were wildly ambitious. He insisted that he would give the Gazette "an interest and a character scarcely claimed by any English Journal even exclusively devoted to literature." He planned to set aside two and a half columns a week for an arts journal that would embrace: essays, translations of German literature and philisophy, statistical tables and an anthology of current

European literature. This was the strategy of a man who, as a missionary of German thought, wanted to spearhead dissemination of the goodword of Kant. "But an Englishman, who knows the infirmity of his own literature," wrote De Quincey, "must acknowledge that in all branches of philosophy, not England only, but all Europe, ought to yield to the precedency of the Germans." In the event, the grand promotion of Kant was limited to two essays in a country that had "yet imported nothing but the coarsest part of the ore" of German literature and philosophy. The first essay, Immanuel Kant and John Gottfried Herder, was an eloquent dismissal of a Chronicle article; and the second, Immanuel Kant and Dr. Herschel, argued the case for philosophic discovery in astronomy and held that Kant had "demonstrated" that Uranus existed, years before the planet was first identified through a telescope by William Herschel.

The promised literary anthology never really got off the ground. De Quincey published a brief sketch of "Monk" Lewis; a biographical essay on Napoleon; poems by John Donne and Thomas Carew; and a few sonnets by Wordsworth, suggested by Westall's views of Yorkshire — but that was all. Ironically, it was only after resigning as Editor that De Quincey produced an article worthy of his declarations. The Danish Origin of the Lake Country Dialect appeared as a four part series in the Autumn of 1819 and was a fine example of linguistic analysis.

As a 'news' paper, De Quincey's Gazette was eminently readable. Outside the political arena, story selection was dictated by the Editor's insatiable appetite for the variety of humanity, and therefore concentrated on people rather than events. The petty frustrations of running a newspaper may have bored De Quincey to distraction, but his basic love of journalism, limitations and all, never diminished. His Editorship of the Gazette confirmed his purpose as a writer; turned his ideas into hard copy for the first time; allowed him to explore his future interests and, above all, rescued him from a stultifying descent into uncontrolled opium abuse. Deadlines and the need to think of others before himself forced De Quincey to impose a degree of order in his life and look outside his private world of hallucination and nightmare. It was a harsh but necessary awakening for a thirty-three-year-old man of limitless potential who had never had a job. Within seventeen months he had proved himself an Editor of qualified success and a journalist of sparkling distinction, destined for better things.

After The Westmorland Gazette, De Quincey languished, unemployed and penniless, in Grasmere. John Wilson came down from Edinburgh late in 1819 and urged him to start contributing articles to Blackwood's Magazine. But De Quincey did nothing and merely drew bills on Wilson to keep his family clothed and fed. Margaret had another baby, a son called Horace, and the De Quinceys left Town End for Fox Ghyll, a house under Loughrigg Fell. By the end of 1820 De Quincey was on his way to Edinburgh, suffering from stomach pains and nausea, and still drawing bills on Wilson. He stayed there six weeks, wrote a few articles for the magazine and left after bickering with Blackwood and Wilson about the lack of copy. De Quincey then headed for London, confirmed in his quest to become a writer for the periodicals. He visited all his old boyhood haunts and defected to Blackwood's arch rival, the London Magazine. He left his lodgings because he could not afford them and spent his time scribbling an essay amid the hectic bustle of coffee houses and coaching inns. In September 1821 that essay, Confessions of an English Opium-Eater, was published in the London Magazine. It was instant fame.

Appendix

"The Danish Origin of the Lake Country Dialect"
The Westmorland Gazette, November 13, 1819.

MR. EDITOR — Rather more than eight years ago I had occasion to learn the Danish language; — in pursuit of what object, I shall mention hereafter; at present I notice it only by way of introducing to your readers a remarkable discovery which I then made — viz. that the dialect spoken in Westmorland and Cumberland, in so far as it is peculiar to those counties, is borrowed wholly from the Danish: for, as a matter of course, one Teutonic language must have some affinity to all others of that family: what I mean — is that all the *words* peculiar to the Lake District at least, and most of the *names* attached to imperishable objects (as mountains, lakes, tarns, &c.) are pure Danish; and in that language only have they uniformly a meaning. Sometimes, it is from the German; and still more frequently from the Icelandic (which indeed is the twin-sister of the Danish). But even in these cases the Danish must be reputed the actual, among several possible, parents of our Cumbrian dialect; because, whilst they severally furnish a key for particular cases here and there, the Danish only furnishes a master key which unlocks nearly all. This fact, I have already said, became known to me first in 1811: three years afterwards I studied the Danish language more closely, and found still further confirmation of it. From history indeed we know that the Danes settled a colony, as in some other parts of England, so especially in "Northumberland," i.e. the county north of the Humber (viz. the six northern counties); and in this as in other cases the evidences of history and language are reciprocal: the records of history lead us to look for the traces of this or that language, and the traces of this or that language confirm the records of history. — Not doubting that your readers will be interested by the fact here brought forward, I shall next week communicate some of the proofs upon which it rests; and, by way of praxis upon my general thesis, I shall apply the Danish language to the particular case of some Westmorland valley — and (according to my former metaphor) I shall compel it to *unlock* the secret meaning of that ancient nomenclature which, with respect to the more permanent features of nature, still survives in the use of the rural population. For the present, — having answered my immediate purpose, which was to fix the attention of your readers more fully by announcing it before hand, — I shall conclude with a short classification of languages in general: I do not offer it as containing anything new to scholars; but it will be interesting to those whose opportunities have not allowed them to investigate this department of knowledge: and moreover it will serve to explain the meaning of the words *Celtic* and *Teutonic* which in my next letter I may now and then have occasion to employ.

Affiliation of Languages. — The languages, spoken upon our planet, may be distributed into three great races —viz. the Oriental, the European, and the Barbarous. 1. By the *Barbarous* I mean all the indigenous languages of America —of Southern and Central Africa — of Northern and Central Asia — of Australasia — Polynesia, &c. It were to be wished that as many as possible of these languages should be examined: for an examination of some has tended to answer one great objection brought against the Mosaical derivation of the human species from common parents: how, it was said, could the islands of the Pacific, &c. have been peopled from any continent — all continents being so remote — during the infancy of navigation? Now on some of the remotest islands the language has been found to be manifestly derived from the (an Asiatic language): and thus the fact that they *were* peopled from a continent is established, be the mode ever so difficult to explain. 2. By the *Oriental* I mean chiefly the languages now spoken throughout the south of Asia — beginning from Arabia, and thence crossing eastwards through a belt of great breadth to China and Japan. This race of languages is very numerous; and, by the exertions of the various Missionaries and of the Bible Society (to whom scholars owe infinite thanks), they are brought more and more within the "field of our glasses"; so that now, sitting in our European studies, we can examine their structure and affinities: in 1813 the Bible was actually translated, or then in a course of translation, into no less than twenty languages between Persia and China. The languages spoken in the great Indian Archipelago must be placed in this or in the preceding class according to the degree of civilization among those who speak it. In this class must be placed also one language spoken in Europe — viz. the Turkish; and more than one spoken in Africa — those which have descended from the ancient Coptic and Ethiopic; and all the Moorish dialects which have diverged from the original language carried along the north coast of Africa by the Saracens (i.e. the Arabs) in the seventh and eighth centuries. To this class belongs also a splendid train of dead languages — as, e.g. the Hebrew, the Syriac, the Chaldee, the Samaritan, the Phenician or Philistine language, and its daughter the Punic or Carthaginian, the Sanscrit or Sungskrita, which is the sacred language of India and used in every part of India. Finally, of this class the Arabic and Persian may be considered the classical languages; in both the literature is extensive: and the numerous MSS. of both which our great English and Continental libraries contain, together with the many aids in the shape of grammars, and dictionaries, make it easy for any European to study them: and with these two languages only has the general scholar any need or any temptation to trouble himself. — Two races being despatched, viz. the Barbarous and the Oriental, we now come to the last and that which most concerns us — viz. the *European*. In this race there are four great families, of which two have intermarried with each other,

— and two have kept themselves wholly distinct. All four have spread themselves from east to west: all four are therefore originally of Asiatic birth. Taking them in the order in which they have succeeded to each other, they stand thus: 1. the Celtic: 2. the Latin: 3. the Teutonic (or Gothic): 4. the Sclavonic. I will go over the chief languages of each family. 1. The Celtic is the most ancient family of all: for, in the time of Julius Caesar (i.e. fifty years before Christ), a Celtic dialect was spoken in Gaul (i.e. throughout France and the Netherlands): and probably the very same language, but certainly a language of the same family, had crept into the *ultima Thule* of Europe — the Britannic Isles: this language subsisted in England for more than four centuries after Christ, when it was gradually driven by Saxon (i.e. Teutonic) tribes into Wales — Cornwall —Cumberland (i.e. the kingdom so called comprehending Westmorland, Cumberland, &c.) — and the kingdom of Strathclwyd. At present this most ancient family of languages is everywhere either decaying or decayed. In the dominions of our own gracious sovereign four Celtic languages are still spoken, and a fifth survives in books: the four living ones are Welch — the Manx — the Irish — and the Gaelic (spoken by the Scotch Highlanders): the fifth, which is orally extinct, is the Cornish: within the memory of some now living we believe there was an old woman in Cornwall who used when angry to scold in Cornish; but she scolded her last, we are told, more than fifty years ago. In Spain there still survives a sixth member of this family — viz. the Basque, spoken in the province (we should say *kingdom*) of Biscay: in France a seventh member — viz. the Armoric or vernacular language of Britanny (Basse Bretagne): and somewhere among the Alps an eighth member, of which I do not recollect the name. These eight languages, we believe, are all of which now remain of the Celtic family of languages; which probably entered Europe three thousand years ago. It has been gradually pushed up by Teutonic incroachers to the very westernmost limits of Europe: and it is remarkable that it nowhere maintains its ground in such perfect security from intrusion as in the absolute west of the old world — viz. in the county of Mayo and other parts of the other province of Connaught, in Ireland. The characteristics of this family, as might be expected, are great simplicity and penury of words unfitting them to express any but elementary thoughts and feelings — and an obstinate repulsion of all other languages, so that no Celtic language has ever blended or amalgamated with any neighbouring language of Teutonic origin. 2. The second family is the Latin: and her four daughters are the Italian, the Spanish, the Portuguese, and the French. I do not mean that they are derived exclusively from the Latin: in all of them some Gothic or Vandal (i.e. Teutonic) dialect — and in the second and third a Moorish or Arabic dialect has furnished the superstructure: but the basis of all is Latin. — The Latin itself is notoriously the child of Æolic Greek by a Celtic mother; at that time the Celtic was younger and less prudish, I suppose, than it has shown itself in later ages. Of Latin I need say nothing: as it is a language of no great compass, so on the other hand it is a language unrivalled for severe and masculine dignity: two centuries ago it was the universal language of scholars throughout Europe: by the laws of the German Empire, which Empire, by the courtesy of Europe, took precedency in Christendom, the Latin language took precedency of all modern languages: no other was to be used in diplomacy: and, if a magnanimous spirit governed the abject statesmen of modern England, we also should refuse to negotiate in the language of our mortal enemy — but, like Cromwell, should compel every nation to approach us either in our own language or in the common language of Europe; but, whatever might suit the feelings of the highminded Cromwell, modern statesmen have instinctively adopted a language, which in point of dignity is on a level with the cackling of poultry or the whinnying of horses, as more in harmony with their own temper and spirit than the language of the Scipios and of Caesar. 3. The third family of languages is the Teutonic; to this belonged of old the languages of all those who from the times of Marius were butting with their horns against the Roman Empire (the Cimbri and Teutones) until they overthrew it and overflowed all its Western Provinces under the name of Heruli — Anglo-Saxons — Ostro-Goths — Visi-

Goths — Vandals, &c. about the fifth century. The original mother is generally supposed to have been the Gothic: of which there is one specimen remaining — viz. the famous Silver Manuscript (so called from its silver letters): it contains the four Gospels and part of the Epistle to the Romans, and is supposed to have belonged to a Gothic Prince as early as the fifth century. This old lady had four daughters, who are now all as dead as herself — viz. the Anglo-Saxon, the Cimbric (otherwise called the Runic), the Frankish, and the Frisic. But, though dead, all these languages have left children behind them. In particular, as we all know, the most illustrious English language is the immediate heiress and representative of the Anglo-Saxon. Some people think that the Anglo-Saxon was not the daughter but the sister of the old Gothic: in which case the Gothic will be aunt to the English: but I believe the fact is as I have represented it — viz. that the old Gothic is our grand-mamma. All the other Teutonic languages are of course our first cousins — viz. the Dutch of Belgic, the German, the Icelandic, and the three Scandinavian languages — i.e. the Danish, the Norse or Norwegian, and the Swedish. The German, I ought to add, is an equivocal word; for there are threé different languages which claim that title — viz. the *Upper* German (Ober Deutsch), spoken in Austria, Suabia and generally in South Germany; the *Lower* German (Nieder Deutsch or Platt Deutsch), spoken in North Germany; and the *High* German (Hock Deutsch), which is spoken all over Germany by people of education, and which has been the sole language of books since the time of Luther. The fourth family of languages is the Sclavonian: this family possesses that whole Eastern region of Europe, and sweeps in a vast zone from Archangel on the Icy Sea to Dalmatia — Istria — Stiria, &c. on the Adriatic, and almost up to the gates of Venice. Of this family the most polished language is by general consent the Russian. — Such is the list, and such the genealogy, of the principal European languages. But there are some anomalous languages which cannot be referred to any one of these four families: I recollect three: first, the Lappish, spoken in Lapland; which is not (as from its situation and political connection one might suppose) a Teutonic language, but a kind of mongrel language which I believe nobody knows anything about unless it be Laplanders and Reindeer. Secondly, the Maltese language; which I believe, is a hybrid language compounded of Arabic and Italian — and therefore well-fitted to occupy the middle station between Christendom and the Mahometan East. Thirdly, the Romaic; and its divine ancestor — the language of Pericles, of Plato and the Euripides: of which the Fathers of the Christian Church did well to affirm —that, if at the day of judgment any human language should be spoke, doubtless it will be Greek.

I remain, Mr. Editor, yours, &c.

K.K.

Nov. 11, 1819.

P.S. I might have added the Latin Family 1. The Lingua Franca, spoken up and down the Mediterranean (especially in the Levant): I believe its basis is Italian. 2. The Occitanique, or language of the Troubadours. 3. The corrupt Latin of Law, &c. in the middle ages.

December 4, 1819

SIR, — With your permission I shall now proceed to establish that proposition which I advanced some weeks back in relation to the dialect of this country. At that time I asserted, as some of your readers may recollect, that the Westmorland dialect does not simply resemble the Danish Language — as English universally resembles Dutch, and as Dutch resembles German; but that in all its peculiarities, i.e. wheresoever it deviates from the general dialect of the north, it is verily and indeed Danish — neither more no less; and that as good Danish will be spoken in Kendal market next Saturday as by any professor at Kiel or Copenhagen. This in substance was the proposition which I then brought forward and promised to make good: and I now proceed (in the pawnbroking phrase of Parliament) to "redeem by pledge".

Let me first however return my thanks to your correspondent UN CLERC for the information which he has so obligingly communicated on the subject of the Gothic MS. discovered at Milan. It is more of his courtesy than of my deserving — that he supposes it to have *'escaped my notice'*, if by that phrase he means that I omitted to notice it from inadvertence: the truth is — I was utterly ignorant that any such discovery had been made: which is the more surprising to myself, inasmuch as I was doubly in the way of knowing it; first from my great attachment to Northern Literature, secondly from the peculiar interest with which I have regarded the other discoveries made of late years in the Milan Library. But so it was: and I have no excuse for myself but this — that I live very much out of the world, and that I have never yet applied myself formally to the study of the old Gothic: what I know of it is through the spectacles of derivative languages: though, by the way, I may add — for the encouragement of those who are meditating to pursue this walk in Literature — that many years ago, when I read no Teutonic language except my own and the High German, I seldom found any difficulty in translating such passages either of the Gothic or of the Frankish (i.e. Teudesque, or Franco-Theotiscan) as I happened to find cited in Dictionaries or Glossaries: it was some assistance to me that I was familiar with the elder literature of England and Scotland in which so many footsteps of the Gothic remain; and some assistance also that I had made myself acquainted with the main joints and hinges of the Gothic and Frankish — such as 'and,' 'for,' 'but,' 'because,' 'if,' 'when,' 'where,' &c: these assistances premised, I am persuaded that no man — being master of the German — will find much more difficulty in reading Gothic than in reading Chaucer; and so intimate is the connection between all the Teutonic languages that he who has acquired any two has already half-mastered all the rest. Indeed I affirm that in eight months a hard student may by adopting a proper method acquire a competent skill in all the living languages descended from the Gothic; in eight months, that is, supposing him a married man; "single gentlemen" in six. — But all this is so much digression from the business which lies before me: briefly then assuring UN CLERC that I shall be happy to profit by any further notes or strictures which may occur to him upon any part of what I advance, I will address myself without further preface to the task I have undertaken — of hunting back the Cumbrian dialect to its Danish original; premising this only — that by the Cumbrian dialect I mean, with reference to my own knowledge of it, chiefly that modification of this dialect which is spoken within the ring-fence of Kendal, Penrith, Keswick, Lorton, Egremont, Coniston, Hawkshead, Burton, Kendal.

Etymology, Mr Editor, is at best a dry subject: and therefore, to enliven it as much as may be, I will introduce my first specimens of Danish in connection with the circumstances under which they draw my attention to the general fact which they illustrate. It was in the hottest part of a very hot day of August in the year 1812 or 1813 that I happened in the course of a long walk to find myself in a sequestered valley of Westmorland: retired from the high road at some little distance, I saw a respectable farmhouse, towards which I turned and begged permission to rest myself within doors for the sake of obtaining a short respite from the oppressive heat of the sun: this being immediately granted with the cheerful courtesy of a Westmorland statesman, I stepped in and took a seat. Whilst the master of the house was conversing with me upon Bonaparte — Marshal Blucher — the National Debt and other like pastoral subjects, I observed in the furthest corner of the house a fine young women sitting with an infant in her lap and busily engaged in playing with it. So entirely was she taken up with her child, that I am afraid she paid very little attention to the wisdom with which we settled the affairs of Europe; and that even the full and clear payment of the National Debt up to the last sixpence, without defrauding a single creditor, failed to give her that satisfaction which at another time no doubt it would have done. Indeed, to say the truth, the loveliness of the youthful mother and child whose joint ages I imagine would not have made eighteen years — their innocent happiness — and the perfect love which appeared to connect them — combined to make up a picture so touching and beautiful — that even I, stoic as I profess myself, could not contemplate it wholly unmoved. My attention being thus drawn to them, I could not fail to hear something of what the mother addressed to her child; and, though all passed in an under voice little above a whisper, I was struck by the words, *"No more Patten"* repeated two or three times and accompanied with a playful gesture as though defending her bosom from the busy little hands of the laughing infant. This word *'Patten'* arrested my notice; for I remembered that *'Patte'* a dissyllable — the *e* final pronounced as the *a* in *sopha* or the e in the French article *le* is the Danish word for a woman's breast. The plural of this word is *"Patten"* — pronounced exactly as it is in Westmorland; and the proper expression (indeed the only expression in Danish for weaning a child — is *'at vaenner et barn fra Patten'* (lit. *to wean a child from the breasts);* in which sentence, as the initial letter in *'vaenner'* is pronounced like a w, a Westmorland man would be at a loss to know whether to call it English or Danish. To be sure that I had heard the word accurately, — I took the liberty of asking the young women what was the meaning of that word *'Patten'* which, if I was not mistaken, she had addressed to her child: hereupon the old 'statesman burst out a laughing; but his granddaughter (as I found she was) blushed and evaded my question by saying it was only a word used to children. I apologised for my freedom by explaining its object; and from the old man I learned my conjecture was right; and since then I have had it frequently confirmed. Such, Mr Editor, was the occasion of my first coming to perceive the Danish origin of the Westmorland dialect; and I have since met with further cases of the same fact in such abundance as would furnish matter for a small Dictionary. Some few of the most striking instances which rest upon my memory I will here adduce. Walking near Ambleside I heard an old woman exclaim "I'll *skyander* him, if he comes here again." I stepped up to her, and conjured her, as she valued the interest of Philology and the further progress of Etymology, that she would expound to me that venerable word (as I doubted not it would prove) which she had just used. "Why," said she, "I'll give him a *serrogle."* This was *'ignotum per ingotus'* with a vengeance: however, I remembered that the Danish word *'skiender'* meant *to scold, to rate,* &c. and on cross-questioning the old woman it appeared that such was the meaning which still bore in Westmorland. "Didn't thee blaspheme my name, and shake thy *neif* in my face at Keswick on Pie Saturday?" said a man at a country fair to another with whom he was wrangling. *'Naev'* (pronounced *neif*) is the Danish word for *fist*: but this word is found south of Westmorland; for it is used by Shakspear. "Master," said a Cumberland girl to me, "Is I to sweep *attercops* off them books?" By *attercops* (as I need scarcely tell your readers, Mr Editor, she meant cobwebs: in Danish 'edderkop' is a spider.

December 18, 1819

'Ost' is the Danish word for *cheese:* in Westmorland it is used to denote cheese before it is put into the press. *'Havre'* is the Danish word for *oats*: with us the univeral name for oaten bread is *havre-cake.* Hence, by the way, comes our national word *'havre-sack'* (i.e. a sack with oats for the horses of the cavalry, as it meant originally). Two Westmorland sisters talking together, I heard the eldest say — "Come, tell me none of those stories from the *'Tantarell's Magazine':"* on inquiry I found that *'tantarell'* meant a gossiper: I have not met with that word in any Danish book; but *'tante'* from which it is manifestly formed, means an idle piece of gossip — a trifling tale. *'Hekkebaertree'*, in some Danish authors, is used to denote the Arbutus: but by elder writers it is used with some latitude of meaning: an Anglo-Danish Dictionary of mine renders it *'a wilding':* in Westmorland it denotes a beautiful shrub of very common occurrence in hedges — which flowers late in the spring and bears a berry: it botanical name I do not know; one of its popular names is the wild cherry-tree. The composition of the Danish word is — *hekke* (hedge) *baer* (berry) *tree* (tree). *'Hekke'* is a common prefix of all wild shrubs: thus *hekke-rose* is the eglantine or common wild rose. With us the word *'heck'* denotes generally a *gate* or *wicket;* perhaps originally a *fence in general. 'Padde'* (a dissyllable) is the Danish word for a *toad: paddock* the Cumbrian. This word by the bye is found in Warwickshire; and Shakspear puts it into the mouth of one of the witches in Macbeth: some of the commentators, either there or in some other place, have explained it to mean a frog: but this is a mistake. In Danish and in Cumbrian alike the word for frog is *'frosk'*. The Danish for mole is *'muldvurp'*, in Cumbrian *'mouldywarp.' Lile* is the universal word with us for little; *lille* the Danish. *Ild* is the Danish word for *fire;* whence with somewhat a pleonasm, the Cumbrians call firing (*i.e.* fuel in general) *fire* — elding. *To lait* is our expression for *'seek'*; the Danish word *leede* to seek (pronounced *laydah*) may be the original. *To 'lake',* which in Cumbrian is *to play,* seems more readily to be derived from the Anglo-Saxon *'lacan'* or the old original Gothic *'laikan'* (which both bear the same meaning) than from the Danish *leege*: but in this, as in many other cases, the present Danish word has supplanted a more ancient one which comes nearer to the Cumbrian; for in the elder Danish writers we find the word *'leyka'* — and never, I think, *'leege.' 'Menseful'* is one of the many words common to the Scotch dialect and that of this country: and it is moreover one of the many which, if the Scotch glossaries are accurate, are used with some difference of acceptation: one of the best Scotch glossaries (that of the late Mr. Sibbald) explains it thus — "menseful, menskful, modest, moderate, discreet, delicate." But in Westmorland I have always heard this word used to express *suitable, becoming* to a man's station in life whatever that might be. Thus for example, I heard a housekeeper say — "That such and such things must be sent for to Kendal, on occasion of a dinner party, to make the table look mensfully set out." Here, Mr. Editor, I will stop to make one general remark: I have observed that, in the history of languages as well as verbal disputes, there has been no more extensive source of errors and of revolutions in the acceptation of words than the substitution of the material for the formal meaning. In this present case Mr. Sibbald was possibly misled in that way: the formal definition of menseful is *decorous, appropriate:* whatsoever realises this meaning will constitute the material definition: but that must vary indefinitely as the particular subject varies. To the condition of a poor man this or the other luxury might be censured by the same epithet: the appearance of things, it might be said, was not menseful: and a stranger might think the word implied the reproach of extravagance in the one case and of parsimony in the mind of the speaker — viz. that which the Romans expressed by the term *convenientia* the French by that of *les convenances.* After all, Mr. Sibbald may not be wrong — even if I am right; for the word may be differently used in Scotland: nor am I sure that my limited experience has taught me the exact use of the word even in Westmorland.

'Fest out' to let out work as the making of shirts &c. Dan. *'faeste'* a lease:

'Faester' to hire or let out.

'Ley' a scythe. Dan. *'lee'* (pronounced lay).

'Teem' to pour out. Dan. *'toemen'* to empty (pronounced *teemen*).

'Sile' to filter. Dan. *'Siilen'* the same. — Asking for a draught of new milk at a farmhouse, I was told that I should have it as soon as it was *'siled'.*

'Kist' a chest. Dan. *'kist'*: and that perhaps from the Greek KISTE.

'Line' flax. Dan. *'liin'*: and that perhaps from the Greek LINON.

'Grave' to dig. Dan. *'graven'* the same.

'Reden' cross — peevish. Dan. *'vreden'* vexed, angry, (the *v* is not pronounced).

'Cope' to exchange — possibly from the Danish *'kioeben'* to buy — (whence, by the way, *Kioben Haven* the Danish name for Copenhagen: or from the old Teutonic 'Koopen' (mercari).

These instances may be sufficient to establish the connection between the Danish and the Cumbrian. What remains of my task, having deferred it to so late a period of the week, I may as well defer to next week; since at this part of the week I fear, Mr. Editor, that you will scarcely find room for what I now send.

January 8, 1820.

SIR, — 1. The Danish origin of the Cumbrian dialect shows itself not merely in a very extensive list of words radically distinct from such as belong to the universal English and wholly unintelligible to a southern Englishman — but also in the peculiar pronunciation of many words common to the Cumbrian and the classical English. E.g. For a *'drunken* man' the Cumbrians say a *'drukken* man'; for 'wr*o*ng' — 'wr*a*ng'; for 'l*o*ng' — 'l*a*ng' (as in *Langdale)*; — all of which, though commonly ascribed to provincial mispronunciation, are good Danish. — Again, for *'sneeze'* the Cumbrians say *'neeze'* — which is the Danish *'nyse'*: for *'home'* they say *'yame'*; at least that comes as near the sound as I can express: — now *'yame'* is the true pronunciation of the Danish word 'hiem' (home). So entirely indeed does the Danish pronunciation survive in some words — that I have remarked (and I have heard others remark), among even well-educated people of Darlington, Stockton, and other places in Durham, the Danish practice of sounding the *k* in words beginning with *kn;* as, e.g., in *'knife'* (Dan. *'kniv'*), *'knee'* (Dan. *'knoe'*), *'kneel'* (Danish *'knaele'*), *'knitting'* (Dan. *'knytting'*): in all which words the people of Stockton &c. sound the *k*; and I think I have remarked the same practice in some persons of education from Penrith (though possibly brought up in Durham). Now this practice is clearly Danish: and so abhorrent to the general usage of England that from earliest times it has been customary to accommodate to the English pronunciation all Danish names beginning with *kn* by intercalating an *a* between the *k* and the *n*. On this principle we say 'King *Can*ute'; whereas the Danish historians call him *'Konge Knud';* which was his real name: and, therefore, it is that our Selden, whose monstrous erudition had mastered every language, ancient as well as modern, from the Euphrates to the Severn, never mentions him by any other name than King *Knout*. Why not King *Knud?* The reader will see below.

2. So richly indeed is our northern vernacular speech interveined with Danish peculiarities, that even the grossest vulgarisms and barbarisms (as we are apt to consider them) cannot safely be condemned for such — until the Danish and its sister dialects have confirmed the verdict. What greater vulgarism, for instance, is there — according to the general feeling of well-educated persons than the common substitute

of 'I *mun*' for 'I *must*'? Yet this is good Icelandic, if not good English; and in earlier times was used by many tribes of those who were called Danes. "Duo defectiva *eg mun* et *eg skal* (i.e. *I mun* and *I shall*), in constructione cum aliis verbis, efficiunt orationis structuram non absimilem illi quam habet Graecorum MELLO: ut *eg mun giöra* vel *eg skal giöra,* Faciam vel Facturus sum." *Ionae Gram. Island.* p.109. —Upon which passage the learned Hickes observes — "*Mun* apud septentrionales Angles et Scotos gerundivam vim habet, conjunctum cum aliis verbis: ut *I mun go,* Abeundum est mihi." — Again, to give another instance, I remember that a young woman from Lancashire, who attended me in my infancy, was accustomed, on any sudden surprise, to exclaim *'Odd rabbit it!';* and I think I have seen the same explanation in some work of l'Estrange's or Tom Brown's. As English, this expression has no meaning: read, therefore on my authority *'Udraabet it', i.e.* literally *'Cry out upon it'* — *'Curse it!' 'Raaben'* in Danish is *to cry* or *ejaculate,* and *'ud'* is the preposition *out:* whence, by the way, *'Outlaw'* in law Latin is '*Ut*legatus' whence also for anology's sake, Selden chose to Anglicize King *Knud* into King *Knout.*

3. Hitherto, Mr. Editor, I have been indebted for my specimens of Danish to the men of Hawkshead, Ambleside, Bowness, &c.; that is, to the Cis-Alpines — as they may be called by those who live on the Windermere side of Kirkstone: but these tribes, though speaking very tolerable Danish for people that have had no Danish schoolmasters during the last eight hundred years, are mere novices in that language — compared with the natives of the Trans-Alpine regions of Patterdale, Matterdale, Martindale, &c. There it is that the Danish is spoken in its purity: there lies our Westmorland-Copenhagen. Amongst the Cis-Alpines are found Danish words in abundance: but in the Trans-Alpine vales the very nerves and sinews of the dialect are Danish: the particles of most common use, the very joints for binding the parts of a sentence together, are Danish: they say *at* for the participle *to;* as, for instance, 'I tell'd him *at* gang yame' for 'I told him *to* go home'. They say 'til' for the preposition *to;* as 'He came *til* me'

for 'He came *to* me'. They say *'fra'* for *from*. They say *'titter'* for *sooner*. They say *'over'* for *'too'*, which indeed is common to all Westmorland: as in the first two lines of a song with which I heard a nurse singing a child to sleep:-

"Bee-bo, Baby-lo! Babies are bonny:
"Two in a bed's enough — three's *over* many."

All are Danish, except, perhaps that *'titter'* comes nearer to Icelandic. In the early Metrical Romances, by the bye, the positive degree *'tyte'*, quick, or soon, is used as commonly as the comparative *'titter'* is in Martindale.

I come now to say a few words on the topographical nomenclature of the Lake district. — In a sublime and very philosophical sonnet Mr. Wordsworth has apostrophised the power of twilight as performing for the external world, as the object of sense, a process analogous to that which he has attributed to the imagination in respect to the world, external or internal, as the objects of thought. Now let us suppose a spectator placed upon the summit of Helvellyn — and that by some process of abstraction *"Day's mutable distinctions"* have been gradually withdrawn from the spectacle below, and only the immutabilities of the scenery preserved; on such a supposition he will have before him a scene the very same which heretofore the ancient Briton or the Dane may have beheld under the same circumstances —

"Those mighty barriers, and the gulph between;
The floods, — the stars, — a spectacle as old
As the beginning of Heavens and Earth."*

Whatsoever then under such circumstances the spectators would see — he may expect to find bearing a British or else a Danish name: the grand barriers of the principal mountains — the great chambers of the valleys which they inclose — the lakes — the streams which feed them at the head, and by which they issue at the foot — all these may be expected to bear ancient names; for these are the ancient features of the scenery — 'the same yesterday, today, and for ever.' But the

*From William Wordsworth's Sonnet XXII.

subordinate incidents of the landscape which belong to the hand of man, and are measured as to duration by his years, — such as woods, and the subdivision of lands, roads, and houses, — will naturally have names coeval with their own origin: and, even where that origin ascends to a very high antiquity, it will sometimes happen with respect to houses and inclosures that the pride of ownership has superseded the ancient name by one more modern — especially where they have been acquired by purchase. Houses, therefore, and inclosures cannot in general be expected to bear Danish names. But to this rule there occur to me at this moment two cases of exception: first, it must be recollected that many houses as well as towns borrow from their localities the same prerogative of immortality which the laws of England attribute to the King: they never die; like Sir Francis Drake's ship, which had been so often repaired that not one of the original timbers remained, there are many houses and towns at this day of which, whilst the materials have perished or been delapidated, the form has been maintained by successive repairs: wheresoever indeed the site of a house or town is peremptorily determined by the relation in which it stands to water or shelter, we may presume the house or the town to be the modern representative of more ancient structures. And it will present a still stronger ground for presuming this if we find reason for believing that second-rate situations were so occupied. If Aa, Ab, Ac, Ad, &c. be a series of homesteads of which the worst is better than the best of the series Ba, Bb, Bc, Bd; then will it be some reason for presuming all the first series to have been occupied in ancient times — if we have sufficient evidence that some of the second series were then occupied. Now this evidence is satisfactorily conveyed in the Danish name which to this day clings to certain houses or homesteads of that description. Here then is one case in which the works of man may, in respect to the perpetuity of their names, share in the privilege usually appropriated to the grandest works of nature—viz. by approaching to nature in her immortality. But there is a second case of exception in which there is no need for supposing any such immortality. — Whosoever is acquainted with the pastoral nomenclature — will know that no figure of speech is of larger influence or more tends to disturb the accuracy of its use and its application than the common figure of synecdoche, by which a part is put for the whole or the whole for a part. Very often the name, which in popular usage is understood to denote a mountain or even a range of mountains, will be restricted amongst learned shepherds to a single point or eminence (just as the name *Holland*, by a natural usurpation over the names of the six confederate states, came to denote all the seven). And *vice versa,* the name of a whole mountain (or even of a cluster of separate heights) will be found in some cases to have settled upon an individual estate or field — and thence upon the house of which they form the little domain. Having premised these general remarks, I will now come more directly to the point; and first I will examine the *Appellatives* of topography (i.e. the general terms of classification under which we arrange the various elements of natural scenery), and secondly a few of the proper names.

Fells, the most comprehensive designation of mountainous grounds, under which as the *genus* are classed the various species of *How, Scar, Crag, &c.* I used to derive it from the German *'Fels'* a rock, but perhaps, it may come from the Danish word *'Feld',* a hill, or mountain.

Dale, from the Danish *'Dal'* a valley; a plank, *i.e.* one of the divisions into which a cubic piece of wood was sawed up; and thence our *Deal* which, from denoting the shapes and relation has come to denote the species of timber; though I believe that timber-merchants still say *Deals* for *Planks.*

Mere, a Lake: I know of no Danish word which it comes so near as the German word 'meer,' a Lake.

Beck, a Brook, or Rivulet: Danish *'Baek',* a Brook.

Holm applied to some of the small island in Windermere: Danish *'Holme',* an Islet: but this word is perhaps a classical English word, and not merely provincial: thus two very remarkable islands in the Bristol Channel are called *The Holms.*

Hawse, any depression or remarkable sinking in a mountainous ridge which allows a road to be carried over it:

thus between Grasmere and Patterdale there is a communication by means of a bridle road carried over a dip at the intersection of Seat — Sandal and Fairfield — either of which mountains at any point would be almost impracticable. This is called *Grisdale Hawse.* Another lies between Little Langdale and Eskdale, Borrowdale and Wastdale, Ennerdale and Buttermere, Long Sleddale and Mardale (at the head of Haweswater) &c. &c. The word is manifestly the word *'Hals'* which both in Danish and German means *a neck:* the mountainous passages being imaged under the relation of a neck to the body of a main mountain. The word *'Hals',* by the way, is common in the old English Metrical Romances under its literal meaning — though never used figuratively as in the Cumbrian. And again, in a whimsical poem entitled *'The Garment of Good Ladies,'* by Robert Henrysoun, a Scotch Poet of the fifteenth century (written, as Lord Hailes had suggested, by way of expanding 1st Tim. chap 2, verse 9, 11) in which he has dressed a young lady out of an allegorical wardrobe:-

Her hat should be of fair *having (i.e. demeanor)*
And her tippet of truth;
Her patelet of good *pansing (i.e. thinking)*
Her HALS-ribbon of ruth.

In which stanza, by the bye, the word *'Patelet',* from which the critics have been unable to explain, may mean her *tucker,* from the Danish *'Patte',* a woman's breast, which I had occasion to cite before. I need scarcely add that the dropping the *l* in *Hals,* as we do in Cumberland, is agreeable to the analogy of most languages in the same case: thus *'fa's'* and *'ca's'* are common in the old Scotch ballads for *falls* and *calls. 'Fawse'* is used for fals: in French *'douce',* sweet, from *dulcis:* the *Malvern* Hills we call *Mawvern: Malham,* near Yorkshire caves, is called Mawn: *Belvoir* Castle, *Bever* Castle. *Tarn,* a small Lake usually lying above the level of the large Lakes and the inhabited dales. — In order to justify the derivation which I am going to suggest for this word I must call the reader's attention to nearer scrutiny of its exact definition. That which I have given above is agreeable to the popular use and meets the case of most tarns as they actually exist: but, if a hair-splitter of logical niceties were to cavil at it, I know not that it would be strictly tenable. To be *above* some dales — is to be *on a level with* others, seeing that their levels are at such various elevations in respect to the sea: and moreover neither of the conditions expressed in the definition is strictly a *sine qua non;* for I presume that, if a lake were much above the neighbouring lakes, it would be called a tarn — even though it were not very small; and again I presume that, if a lake were a very small one, it would be called a tarn — even though it were not above the level of the neighbouring lakes; indeed this latter presumption is realised in the case of Blellam Tarn, a small lake between Ambleside and Hawkshead, and also in that between Carlisle and Hesketh. Thus then it appears that the definition cannot be a good one, because it does not reciprocate with the thing defined; for, though every small lake above other lakes is a tarn, yet every tarn is not a small lake above others. But, though it is not impregnable as a definition, it may answer pretty well as a description of the general circumstances, which combine to constitute a tarn: and it will answer the better if to these we add one other which was pointed out to me by Mr. Wordsworth. That gentlemen whose severe accuracy of logic is well known to those who have the honour of his acquaintance, once remarked to me in conversation — that, whereas lakes have always one main feeder, of tarns on the contrary it is characteristic that they are fed by a multitude of small independent rills all apparently equal in importance; or (it may be added) having only a transient pre-eminence according to the accidental inequalities in the distribution of mountain showers (which are often confined to spots of a few square yards) and of snow in both respect to the very various dimensions of the areas which melt into any one rill, and also to the very different accumulations of it by driftings, as governed by the wind and the circumstances of the ground. Thus discriminated then the tarn will be rather a deposition or settling of water from the little rain-rills converging from the steep banks immediately adjacent, whilst a lake will be the disemboguing of a river after it has collected many inferior streams into a spacious bed or area not necessarily surrounded by precipitous banks. With this preface I shall now venture to derive the word from the Danish word *Taaren,* a trickling of gradual deposition.

Bibliography

1818 — 1819 The Westmorland Gazette, and accounts book.

1818 — 1819 The Westmorland Advertiser and Kendal Chronicle.

1818 Harrison T., An Impartial Narrative of the Riotous Proceedings which took place on Wednesday February 11th, 1818 Airey and Bellingham, Kendal.

1832 Nicholson, Cornelius, The Annals of Kendal, Whitaker and Co., London.

1889 — 1890 Masson, David, ed., Collected Writings of Thomas De Quincey, 14 vols, A. and C. Black, Edinburgh.

1890 Pollitt, Charles, De Quincey's Editorship of The Westmorland Gazette July 1818 to November 1819, Atkinson and Pollitt, Kendal.

1895 Hogg, James, ed., De Quincey and His Friends, Sampson Low and Marston, London.

1900 Curwen, John, Kirkbie Kendall, T. Wilson, Kendal.

1909 Noble, S. C., The Kendal Newsroom, Atkinson and Pollitt, Kendal.

1916 Armitt, Mary L., Rydal, ed. Willingham F. Rawnsley, Titus Wilson, Kendal.

1932 Hammond J. L. and B., The Village Labourer 1760 — 1832, Longmans, Green and Co, Ltd. London.

1936 Eaton, H. A., Thomas De Quincey: A Biography, OUP, London.

1940 Wells, John Edwin, Wordsworth and De Quincey in Westmorland Politics, 1818, PMLA, vol LV, no. 4.

1948 Douglas, Wallace W., Wordsworth in Politics: The Westmorland Election of 1818, MLN, vol XLIII, no. 7.

1956 — 1971 Griggs, E. L., ed., Collected Letters of Samuel Taylor Coleridge, Routledge and Kegan Paul, London.

1961 Bouch, C. M. L., and G. P. Jones, The Lake Counties 1500 — 1830, A Social and Economic History, Manchester University Press.

1961 New, Chester W., The Life of Henry Brougham to 1830, Clarendon Press, Oxford.

1962 Jordan, John E., De Quincey to Wordsworth: A Biography of a Relationship, University of California Press.

1965 Moorman, Mary, William Wordsworth: A Biography, The Later Years 1803 — 1850, Clarendon Press, Oxford.

1965 Brown, P.A. The French Revolution in English History, Frank Cass and Co. Ltd, London.

1966 Stern, Philip Van Doren, ed., Thomas De Quincey, Selected Writings, Nonesuch Press, London.

1968 Janzow, F. S., De Quincey Enters Journalism: His Contributions to the Westmorland Gazette 1818 — 1819, doctoral dissertation, University of Chicago.

1970 Selincourt, Ernest De., ed., revised Mary Moorman and Alan G. Hill, The Letters of William and Dorothy Wordsworth III The Middle Years part two 1812 — 1820, Clarendon Press, Oxford.

1970 Wright, David ed., Recollections of the Lakes and Lake Poets, Thomas De Quincey, Penguin.

1973 Moran, James, Printing Presses, History and Development from the fifteenth century to modern times, Faber and Faber Ltd, London.

1973 Aspinall, A., Politics and the Press c. 1780 — 1850, Harvester Press, Brighton.

1973 Salaman, Esther, The Great Confession, Allen Lane, The Penguin Press, London.

1974 Sackville West, Edward, ed., John Jordan, A Flame in Sunlight: The Life and Work of Thomas De Quincey, Bodley Head, London.

1974 Lefebure, Molly, Samual Taylor Coleridge, A Bondage of Opium, Victor Gollancz Ltd, London.

1975 Cipolla, Carlo M., ed., Economic History of Europe, Collins, Glasgow.

1978 Wordsworth, William, ed., Thomson Hutchinson, revised Ernest De Selincourt, Poetical Works, OUP.

1980 Davies, Hunter, William Wordsworth, Weidenfield and Nicholson Ltd, London.

1980 MacPherson C. B., ed., Thomas Hobbes: Leviathan, Penguin.

1981 Lindop, Grevel, The Opium-Eater: A Life of Thomas De Quincey, J. M. Dent and Sons Ltd.

1983 Sales, Roger, English Literature in History 1780 — 1830 Pastoral and Politics, ed., Raymond Williams, Hutchinson, London.

References

Girlish Tears

1. Masson I, 32.
2. Masson I, 277/278.
3. Masson I, 32.
4. Masson I, 33.
5. Masson I, 42.
6. Masson I, 45.
7. Masson I, 36/37.
8. Sackville West, 24.
9. Masson I, 25/26.
10. Masson I, 21.
11. Masson I, 59.
12. Masson I, 65.
13. Masson I, 85.
14. Masson I, 103/104.
15. Masson I, 110.
16. Masson I, 110.
17. Masson I, 152.
18. Van Doren Stern, 305.
19. Lindop, 28.
20. Masson I, 181/182
21. Masson I, 198.
22. Masson I, 209
23. Japp, 37
24. Sackville West, 31.
25. Masson I, 342.
26. Masson I, 327.
27. Masson I, 377.
28. Masson III, 249.

On the Road

1. Lindop, 124.
2. Masson III, 338.
3. Masson III, 346.
4. Masson III, 346.
5. Masson III, 347.
6. Masson III, 360.
7. Masson III, 375.
8. Masson III, 375.
9. Lindop, 99.
10. Lindop, 102.
11. Jordan, 29.
12. Jordan, 29.
13. Jordan, 20.
14. Sackville West, 64.
15. Masson II, 60.
16. Masson II, 55.
17. Masson II, 86.
18. Westmorland Gazette, June 26th, 1819.
19. Westmorland Gazette, May 8th, 1819.
20. Masson III, 381.

Greeting the Dark Interpreter

1. Kirkbie Kendall, 165.
2. Griggs, III, 49.
3. Masson III, 388.
4. Masson III, 388/389.
5. Masson III, 389/390.
6. Salaman, 57.
7. Stern, Philip van Doren, 906.
8. Masson III, 392/393.
9. Masson III, 394.
10. Jordan, 24.
11. Masson II, 150.
12. Masson II, 152/153.
13. Masson II, 146.
14. Masson II, 243.
15. Masson II, 238.
16. Masson II, 239.
17. Masson II, 240.
18. Masson II, 285.
19. Masson II, 188.
20. Jordan, 87.
21. Jordan, 87/88.
22. Masson II, 192.
23. Masson II, 192.
24. Jordan, 58.
25. Moorman, Wordsworth Letters, Middle Years, 351.
26. Moorman, Letters, 347.
27. Moorman, biography, 147.
28. Moorman, Letters, 350.
29. Eaton, 158.
30. Jordan, 178.
31. Moorman, Letters, 357.
32. Masson III, 99.
33. Jordan, 204

For Better or Worse

1. Masson II, 287.
2. Massson II, 287.
3. Jordan, 50.
4. Wordsworth, Poetical Works, 735.
5. Masson V, 268.
6. Masson II, 384.
7. Masson XIII, 351.
8. Masson II 387.
9. Masson II, 389.
10. Jordan, 219.
11. Masson XIII, 131.
12. Westmorland Gazette, December 4th, 1819.
13. Hogg, 156.
14. Masson II, 209.
15. Masson XIII, 14.
16. Masson XIII, 14.
17. Masson XIII, 349.
18. Jordon, 266.
19. Eaton, 210.
20. Salaman, 46.
21. Masson II, 445.
22. Moorman, Letters, 80.
23. Masson III, 200.
24. Masson III, 198.
25. Masson III, 199.
26. Masson III, 204.
27. Masson III, 206.
28. Wright, 186.
29. Wordsworth MSS.
30. Moorman, Letters, 372.
31. Eaton, 220.
32. Eaton, 282/283.
33. Jordan, 233.
34. Masson III, 442.

Government Property and High Tories

1. Brown, 209.
2. Hunt, Leigh, Feast of the Poets, 1815, 99.
3. Moorman, Letters, 375/376.
4. Wordsworth, Poetical Works, 22.
5. Moorman Letters, 406.
6. Moorman, biography, 345.
7. Coburn, 132.
8. Moorman, Letters, 449
9. Douglas, Wallace, pamphlet.
10. Lowther MSS, Carlisle.
11. Lowther MSS, Carlisle.
12. Moorman, Letters, 419.
13. Moorman, Letters, 425
14. Moorman, Letters, 427.
15. Moorman, Letters, 433.
16. Gazette accounts book.
17. Chronicle, February 28th, 1818.
18. Chronicle, February 28th, 1818.
19. Lowther MSS, Carlisle.
20. Wordsworth MSS.
21. Wordsworth MSS.
22. Wordsworth MSS.
23. Moorman, Letters, 438.
24. Chronicle, March 28th, 1818.
25. Moorman, Letters, 444.
26. Chronicle, March 27th, 1818.
27. Moorman, Letters, 464.
28. Wells, Edwin, PMLA, vol XLIII, no 7.
29. Wordsworth MSS.

Newspaper at War

1. Gazette, May 23rd, 1818.
2. Gazette, May 23rd, 1818.
3. Gazette, May 23rd, 1818.
4. Gazette, May 30th , 1818.
5. Chronicle, June 20th, 1818.
6. Chronicle, June 20th, 1818.
7. Chronicle, June 6th, 1819.
8. Moorman, Letters, 468.
9. Lowther MSS.
10. De Quincey MSS, Kendal Records Office.
11. Gazette accounts book.
12. Lowther MSS.
13. Moorman, Letters, 478.
14. Wordworth MSS.
15. Gazette, July 11th, 1818.
16. Gazette, July 18th, 1818.
17. Masson IX, 331/332.
18. Masson IX, 349.
19. Moran, 54.
20. Aspinall, 28.
21. Noble, 3.
22. Gazette, December 26th, 1818.
23. Gazette, August 29th, 1818.
24. Chronicle, September 5th, 1818.
25. Leviathan, 181.
26. Jordan, 324.
27. Gazette, October 3rd, 1818.
28. Wordsworth MSS.
29. Moorman, Letters, 489.
30. Moorman, Letters, 492.
31. Wordsworth MSS.
32. Wordsworth MSS.
33. Moorman, Letters, 497.
34. Gazette, March 20th, 1819.
35. Wordsworth MSS.
36. Wordsworth MSS.
37. Moorman, Letters, 511.
38. Gazette, November 28th, 1818.
39. Gazette, November 21st, 1818.
40. Masson III, 441.
41. Gazette, December 12th, 1818.
42. Masson IX, 316.
43. Gazette, January 23rd, 1819.
44. Gazette, January 9th, 1819.
45. Masson III, 432.
46. Masson III, 432.

47. Masson III, 433.
48. Gazette, April 17th, 1819.
49. Gazette, April 3rd, 1819.
50. Gazette, March 27th, 1819.
51. Gazette, April 17th, 1819.
52. Moorman, Letters, 544.
53. Gazette, March 20th, 1819.
54. Pollitt, 43.
55. Gazette, April 24th, 1819.
56. Gazette, June 19th, 1819.
57. Gazette, June 12th, 1819.
58. Chronicle, July 3rd, 1819.
59. Chronicle, July 3rd, 1819.
60. Jordan, 326.
61. Gazette, August 28th, 1819.
62. Gazette, November 6th, 1819.
63. Gazette, accounts book.
64. Lowther MSS.
65. Moorman, Letters, 608.
66. Lowther MSS.
67. Lowther MSS.
68. Lowther MSS.
69. Masson III, 433.

The Babbling Garrulity of Daylight

1. Gazette, January 30th, 1819.
2. Chronicle, February 6th, 1819.
3. Jordan, 324.
4. Gazette, January 9th, 1819.
5. Gazette, January 23rd, 1819.
6. Gazette, August 8th, 1819.
7. Gazette, September 12th, 1818.
8. Chronicle, December 12th, 1818.
9. Gazette, December 12th, 1818.
10. Masson XIII, 46.
11. Masson X, 391/392.
12. Masson X, 389.
13. Masson XIII, 12.
14. Gazette, November 28th, 1818.
15. Gazette, December 5th, 1818.
16. Gazette, January 30th, 1819.
17. Gazette, July 25th, 1818.
18. Gazette, January 2nd, 1819.
19. Gazette, November 28th 1818.
20. Gazette, January 23rd, 1819.
21. Gazette, April 24th, 1819.
22. Gazette, July 17th, 1819.
23. Gazette, January 2nd, 1819.
24. Gazette, September 5th, 1818.
25. Masson III, 405.
26. Masson III, 443.
27. Gazette, March 27th, 1819.
28. Masson XIII, 286/287.
29. Masson XIII, 289.
30. Masson II, 356.
31. Masson XIII, 317.
32. Masson XIII, 329.
33. Masson XIII, 304.
34. Gazette, August 7th, 1818.
35. Masson I, 102.